Always on a S

An Englishman in Greece

Brian Church

Athens News

ISBN 960-86395-2-2

Printed and bound in Athens, Greece by Lambrakis Press S.A.
Pre-press by Multimedia S.A.

To the millions of Athenians
who have had water dropped
on their heads in the street.

(One day we'll get them, my friends, one day.)

CONTENTS

Author's Preface xi
Acknowledgements xiii

CHAPTER ONE
Engine of the Madhouse (Welcome to Athens) 1

1. Athenians Anonymous
Don't worry, you're not alone 3

2. Athens Airport
A new capital takes off 9

3. Athens News
Tales from the South Pacific 12

4. Athens Metro
Very nice but why is it underground? 15

5. Piraeus
We're not in Athens 18

CHAPTER TWO
The Unforgettable Greece 21

6. People Power
Best thing about Greece? Greeks 23

7. Food for Thought
Religion, identity and yoghurt 27

8. A Fright at the Theatre
Final curtain comes down on one critic 30

9. Greek Police
Red trousers at night, copper's delight 33

10. Earthquakes
How to predict them after they've happened 36

CHAPTER THREE
The War of Words & The Words of War 39

11. The Balkans
Where are they? 41

12. Ocalan and Imia
Trust & treason 45

13. Diplomacy, Poker and Mrs Campbell
Playing chess in front of the world 48

14. November 17
Europe's thickest terrorists 51

15. The Eurovision Song Contest
Rhymes against humanity 54

CHAPTER FOUR
An Interview With the Earl of Elgin (and Other 'Criminals') 57

16. The Earl of Elgin
Sometimes I wish he'd never taken them 59

17. Garry Kasparov
Yes? 64

18. Michael Dukakis
It wasn't the best of campaigns 66

19. Gerry Adams
I've never killed anyone 69

20. Richard Branson
Perhaps I should be more ambitious 72

CHAPTER FIVE
A Long Way From High Wycombe: Travels Around Greece 75

21. Kareas
Putting problems in perspective 77

22. Kos
Little Ben, Big Ben 81

23. Corfu
If you've time for only one island, this is it! 84

24. Chios
Mastic, Homer and Muhammad Ali 85

25. High Wycombe
Home of the Windsor Chair 87

CHAPTER SIX
What's the Hurry? (Good Things Come to Those Who Wait) 93

26. The 2004 Athens Olympics
You ain't seen nothing yet! 95

27. Rejection
Women hurt but articles wound 99

28. Greek TV
Turning the nation on 102

29. Some Day My Bus Will Come
Adam and Eve on tour 105

30. Queen of the Chocolate Drops
Loyalty on legs 108

AUTHOR'S PREFACE

Life in England. Life in Greece. What's the difference?

London is obviously a lot wetter than Athens. Transport is ten times as expensive. There's far more crime. Worst of all, England is distressingly predictable.

Before coming out to Greece, my sheltered life was so dull and limited that I had *never* experienced any of the following: Wall-wobbling earthquakes, plagues of flies, police searching me at gunpoint, giant cockroaches, raw sewage spewing into my living room, a dog landing in front of my eyes after falling from two floors above ('Excuse me, your dog's just dropped off the balcony') and neighbours getting trapped in the lift, collapsing into the flower bed or screaming abuse at each other before going off laughing and arm-in-arm for a coffee.

And I live in a really quiet area of Athens.

Always on a Sunday tries to show what goes on in Greece during the rest of the week. Everything presented as fact is indeed true (or true hearsay). In October 1997, the wife of a man who chopped up his schizophrenic son honestly did say out loud in court: 'I wonder what it is we're living through. I ask myself: Is it fate? Or is it the enigma of life as mentioned by Dostoyevsky?'

In England, such a statement from the witness box would cause the case to collapse since no jury, judge or journalist could henceforth keep a straight face. Education is more prized here and many readers will notice this book's total lack of 'culture'. Not even *Captain Corelli's Thingamabob*. For this English philistine, true culture is gazing in wonder at the Acropolis as I walk home from the supermarket and staring at the supermarket as I climb up the Acropolis. It sure is a beautiful feeling, especially when they've got an offer on tuna.

Actually, I've never been to the top of the Acropolis. I vowed on first coming here that I would only take the lift to the Parthenon with a little daughter or son by my side. Knowing my luck, they'll probably have moved it by the time that happens. But it's been a nice thought to have kept me company all these years, some of which were longer than others.

Here's another confession. Much of *Always on a Sunday* is what you read word for word in the *Athens News* weeks, months or years ago and have now forgotten. But some of the original articles have been blended, many posthumously chopped or enlarged, and a few rewritten. The interviews and travel features weren't even for *Church on Sunday,* and a couple of pieces – the Corfu special report for example (Page 84) – are appearing in print for the very first time.

The problem throughout was to make the text flow, often removing references to specific days of the week and eliminating important but now obscure events, such as my 30th birthday, or indeed jokes. Take this (surely unoriginal?) jibe from 30 January 1994 which revealed that customs at Athens Airport had three large signs on display: *Nothing to declare, Something to declare* and *Mr Constantine Mitsotakis.* Just not funny if you didn't know that, at the time, the former New Democracy prime minister was being relentlessly accused of stockpiling illegal antiquities.

Where I could be bothered, there are notes to update the situation at the end of an article. Ages and titles are correct as of the date given in the introduction. Outrageous or offensive questions attributed to the *Athens News* in the original reports (and hence this book) are mine. All these additions and subtractions, bar none, are intended to make you think that *Church on Sunday* is a weekly beacon of outstanding satire and for that reason you should buy this book. It isn't. You have. Sorry.

Most importantly, *Always on a Sunday* lets me put on record my utter adoration for both the Greek people and their great nation. I have long treated Greece like another country I love, The Republic of High Wycombe, Home of the Windsor Chair (see Page 87), praising wherever possible and criticising only when necessary – and even then with affection and restraint. A voluntary witness since 1992, I can personally testify there's an awful lot more to admire in Greece than attack. The same goes for Scotland, the gracious recipient of various light-hearted remarks in this book, and to a lesser extent Syntagma Post Office.

Brian Church
High Wycombe
(Home of the Windsor Chair)
December 2001

ACKNOWLEDGEMENTS

This book was written in extreme haste and at minimal effort so as to keep the original spirit of *Church on Sunday* which has disgraced many different pages of the *Athens News* since October 1993.

Originally appearing every Sunday, the column's clever name was suggested by the elongated Derek Gatopoulos. Well done Derek.

Name aside, a key explanation for the durability of *Church on Sunday* – the paper's longest-running feature after *Items for Sale* in the classified ads – is that I have never underestimated just how stupid most of my regular readers are. Market research shows that when the column has been moved to a different page, a whopping two thirds of *ConS* fans can't find it. Many of them will be puzzled by this book's title, which derives from the classic Melina Mercouri film, *Cat on a Hot Tin Roof.* But they're fanatically loyal, reading me in streets, prisons and slum areas around the world, and I quite sadly owe them everything.

The *Athens News* has been a wonderful place to throw away my entire career. Particular thanks to the Editor, John Psaropoulos, for accepting this humble offering which happily turned out only a few pages shorter than he had originally asked for. I hope to be out of the country when he first notices Page 37 is followed by Page 138.

Many a John looked at different parts of the manuscript. If John Hadoulis, John Chorny, (Big) John Ross (King of the Beach) and John the Boss made any helpful suggestions, I didn't see them but they meant well.

Quality observation, factual info, general advice or total disassociation came from Philip Pangalos, Romolo Gandolfo, Christy Papadopoulou, Nicholas Paphitis, Demetris Nellas, Dinos Mitsis, Maria Paravantes, Eddie Brannigan, cousin Djordje Crncevic, sister Sue Williams, sister-in-law Paul Williams, Angeliki Contes and, in order of size, Giraffe Gatopoulos, normal-height Trouble Bozaninou and the inch-starved Paris 'I agree with myself on this issue' Agiomamitis, who once escaped a storm in Japan by sheltering under a bonsai tree. As ever, all opinions are mine and the many mistakes left in are theirs. Debbie Ellis from Wales speed-read the manuscript on the London-Cardiff motorway.

Production and layout wizards Constanza Miliou and, particularly, Nikos Kollias were a joy to work with. So too Jenny Kosma and Maria Angelopoulou, from the Athens News, who have been put in this world to solve any post-publication problems with my books. This is an often thankless task which they carry out with admirable hard work and graceful intimidation.

CHAPTER ONE

Engine of the Madhouse (Welcome to Athens)

A Greek president once said
his country was a giant asylum.
Guess where most of the patients live.

Athenians Anonymous

Don't worry, you're not alone

Countless Athenians over thousands of years have fallen for the same trap: 1) Water drops on your head. 2) You look up. 3) You fall down a hole in the street.

Greece makes people happier. Athens makes them stranger. And wetter.

Only when you have become as damp and weird as the average Athenian and begin to find normal people curious, dry even, do you start to fall in love with the place. The process can take from five minutes to 50 years. Ironically, when you return to your original country for good, months will pass before you get used to *not* having 'water' falling on you from above (reputedly from air conditioners).

Foreign motorists are among the first to readjust to Athens, their very survival being at stake. If you've never driven here, take this test. The traffic lights are red, and you've stopped at a crossroads. Here you see a *No left turn* sign and a policeman blocking entry on the right. In how many different directions can you go? In most of the world the answer would be *none* because the lights are red, remember? In Greece, the answer is of course *five*: Straight on (the light's green), turn right (what policeman?), turn left (who says you can't?), U-turn and high-speed reverse.

Crossroads are also a good opportunity for pedestrians to admire all the different objects – bikes, ladders, bookcases, mattresses, speedboats, etc – being held down on the car roof by the driver and his front-seat passenger simply sticking their hands out of the window.

Perhaps they'd been shopping. Even here, you must concentrate. There is a bizarre tendency for shops to tell you exactly when they're closed rather than ever reveal their actual opening hours. A typical sign in the summer reads: CLOSED FOR THE MONTH OF AUGUST. WE REOPEN NOVEMBER 7. In a similar vein, the 24-hour taverna in Piraeus was shut at 3am the night I visited and the 'Everything for 297 drachmas' shop in Exarcheia had a nice-looking radio for 2,497 drachmas.

Note also the obsession with having the correct change. I long to use my 500-billion-dinar note from Serbia in a supermarket just to hear the cashier complain, 'Don't you have anything smaller?' The problem is not here in Greece but when you try to take the custom home with you and cause mass confusion by offering to pay an English bill of 8.75 with 14.25 in order to get a five-pound note and a 50-pence piece back.

Greece joined the Euro-Zone on 1 January 2001 and this great change debate is going to get even more complicated with the launch of the euro in 2002. The first reference I ever saw to Greece's new currency was the food delivery service, Eurolunch.

What else can you expect in the land of the unexpected? Occasional electricity cuts, usually very brief, half a minute say, but as often as once or twice a week. Being very poor at paying bills on time, my immediate reaction is always to rush outside my flat and press the 'Call lift' button to see if it's only my apartment affected, ie the power will stay off. That feeling of relief on hearing the 98-year-old trapped inside and screaming two and a half floors up is hard to describe.

Athens is teeming with paradoxes. Greek homes are exceptionally clean and the roads dreadfully dirty. The noisiest capital in Europe is also the most peaceful, with no drunks and no fights, though more street, office and home arguments than you could ever imagine. Animals have long been treated dreadfully, poisoned even, but many, especially the young, adore cats and dogs.

A virulent anti-Americanism is accompanied by a deep interest in all things American (one homegrown comedy sketch showed some shepherds discussing the performance of the hi-tech Nasdaq stock market). The US State Department says it spends more on protecting its diplomats here than anywhere else in the world, yet, apart from dieting, violence is the most un-Greek activity imaginable (I saw one surreal sign at the British embassy in Athens: *This fire door must remain open unless the building is being attacked*).

More paradoxes: One of the freest societies around is not particularly creative, overflowing with unknown 'internationally famous' artists. There's a lot of verbal racism but not the corresponding degree of ill-treatment seen in much of Europe. Greeks are nationalists yet generous hosts to many foreigners.

Tradition spars with modern-day needs. I watched the *evzones* walk from the president's palace to their permanent guard outside parliament, closely followed, as always, by a military escort. They walked past a kiosk. Or at least the *evzones* did. The escort stopped to get a packet of cigarettes.

The biggest paradox is the huge number of laws and their almost total non-enforcement – one reason why Greeks are so heavily in favour of the EU is because there are few negative consequences. Sometimes you wish a few laws were kept. Around one tourist attraction, there's a shop which by law sells bottled water at controlled prices, hugely sensible given the summer heat. But they've 'run out' the last two times I've been there and you're forced to buy another drink at least twice the price.

Athens in the 21st century is changing at a much faster rate than before. Even Syntagma Post Office, previously so slow that the police asked for advice on crowd control, has a new system at work. You go in, press a button on a machine, get the ticket 2187 and start making plans for your youngest great-great-great-grandson to pay the phone bill until realising this is a cumulative number throughout the week and you're about to be served. No you're not, she's having a coffee. And it *is* a she.

In politics, which is forever Athens-based, actual moderation, as opposed to relative moderation, is now becoming a real force for perhaps the first time in modern Greek history. Both the current prime minister, Costas Simitis (in office for a magnificent six years, come the end of January 2002, though living with a troublesome party and an electorate at times keen on a change of ruling party but not premier), and President Costis Stephanopoulos (re-elected for a second five-year term in March 2000) have shown on many occasions that you can stand up for your country without inciting hatred of foreigners or wearing a black hat.

The leadership of the Orthodox Church of Greece occasionally appears to be mind-numbingly nationalist (in stark contrast to Orthodoxy's worldwide 'boss', the deeply admirable Ecumenical Patriarch Vartholomeos), and seemingly unconcerned with the day-to-day life of the poor, much like myself in fact, so I shouldn't be too critical.

Simitis, born in 1936, has tried hard for much of his life to modernise Greece. A nationwide general strike in April 2001 rather pettily protested against his government's commendable plan to take everybody's pension away. The revolutionary scheme, hastily abandoned, required employees to work for 40 whole years before being able to draw a full pension. Statisticians worked out that some Syntagma Post Office employees wouldn't be entitled to their pensions until 2715.

Some things stay the same. Unchanging and real family values, lived out every day despite the stresses and strains, top any list of what makes Athens a classy place to live in. When my father was injured in a car accident and I wanted to go back to England, it was not only easy to get time off but *expected* that I would go.

On a simpler level, make yourself a salad, with fresh veg from the local market, have a Greek coffee and sit on the balcony with a newspaper. Listen out as well for the QGs, the Quiet Greeks, a rare species, but some of the very best Hellenes in town, constantly amused by their fellow countrymen, sometimes embarrassed.

As you will be. You have to quickly adjust to the lack of privacy and the outstanding rudeness of some people when they shove you out of the way, jump a queue, or delay an entire plane and then try to justify why they were late. Don't judge too harshly. This is just them playing the game. They wouldn't do this in Texas, where they would be instantly shot.

But here in the Lone Taxpayer State, there is no such thing as inexcusable behaviour and no one is ever responsible for anything. Some foreigners just can't stand it and there are more than a few for whom this book will bring back only bad memories. Please send them a copy.

But you've got to laugh. Culture, archaeology and all the other mandatory mentionables aside, Athens remains an extraordinary society, and that includes the window cleaner two big floors up, back to the road, no safety attachments, probable death if he falls. He never does, even when I ask him the time.

Every day the capital puts on one big, free performance. Athens might be incredibly noisy, hot and chaotic but give the place time and you'll discover the city's a big softy. Safe, fun, great food, lovely people when you get to know them and the strongest anti-diarrhoea tablets in the European Union. What more could you ask for?

◪ English-language newspapers in Greece are often forced to insert (sic) into their reports to reassure readers, 'Hey, we couldn't believe this story either but it's true!' Here's my own Top Ten from the past decade, some funny, a few tragic, and all totally true:

10 Vangelis Rohamis escaped from prison for the sixth time (sic) in August 1994. The *Athens News* used the occasion to caustically note: 'Last year [1993] he was granted a five-day leave from which he unexpectedly returned.' Perhaps the heat's to blame. In August 2001, Costas Passaris, the country's most-wanted fugitive, managed to escape from his second-floor hideout (after being ordered to surrender), flee down the stairs (sic) and disappear in front of a reported 50 (sic) heavily armed police officers, 'including members of an elite unit' (Associated Press). Passaris was caught by his dog four months later in Romania.

9 A road safety crackdown in June 1998 is forced to point out that 'reversing on a motorway' (sic) remains an offence, punishable by a 100,000-drachma fine.

8 Saturday morning, 4 November 2000. Christos Kendiras, 49, wakes up, has a coffee, murders his mother-in-law and his wife's alleged lover, then hijacks a busload of Japanese tourists (sic). To the Greek police's great credit, they don't shoot him. To the Greek police's great discredit...see Note a), Page 104, for what happened next. Japanese tourists have had a tough time in Greece. In their September 2001 story, *'Cookie-wielding' thief arrested,* the English *Kathimerini* reported that a Moroccan man had been arrested for allegedly offering 'biscuits containing ground-up sleeping tablets' to visitors at archaeological sites and then robbing them when they had fallen asleep. Mostly Japanese tourists accepted.

7 POLICE! DROP YOUR FRUIT NOW. On Friday 26 January 2001, 43-year-old Aristidis Mouratidis threatened to blow up a bank in Alexandroupolis, northeastern Greece, with what turned out to be a bag of apples, type unknown. He was arrested by cops from the main police station just 50 metres away. On 12 June 2001, tipped off about 220 million drachmas ($550,000) stuffed in two mail bags, 'five hooded robbers held up an Athens post office and took off with hundreds of algebra, Latin and chemistry exam papers' (Reuters).

6 Furious at a referee's decision, Panionios basketball star Boban Jankovic whacked his head against a metal post in protest and collapsed on court. He has been paralysed since then – early 1992.

5 A couple in Thessaloniki received a water bill, June 1996, for 262,694,000 drachmas, then around a million dollars. It was thought to be the biggest water bill ever issued in Greece since a Scotsman in Glyfada discovered his local supermarket sold home brewing kits. The EYDAP office said the bill, which should have been a more reasonable 3,100 drachmas, was the result of a 'typing error' (sic).

4 Two managers from Swedish telecommunications giant Ericsson arranged in February 2000 for a pair of hooded gunmen (sic) to stop and board a staff bus travelling from Athens to Corinth. The managers, a Greek and a Finn, apparently wanted to see how their employees would cope in a crisis (sic). It all backfired spectacularly when a member of the public saw the incident and, ironically, used his mobile phone to call the police.

3 In November 1993, Athens daily *Apoyevmatini* mixed up US country & western singer-actor Kris Kristofferson with the man they meant to attack, EC economic affairs commissioner Henning Christophersen.

2 June 2000, Kalambaka, central Greece. 'A convicted axe murderer recently released from prison for killing her son was arrested on Friday for hacking her husband to death in a pigsty...Her other son died in a traffic accident on the way to his brother's funeral' (AP report).

1 This one's immortal. On 14 November 1998, a group of Kurds started a hunger strike in Athens' Klafthmonos Square in protest at the arrest in Rome of PKK leader Abdullah Ocalan. Some ten days later, and in the very same square, a private company and a cookery school made a joint world record attempt at baking the largest ever profiterole (sic). Noting some observers' complaints of bad taste, the *Athens News* said the giant pastry weighed 'almost five tonnes' and was 'topped with half a tonne of whipped cream'. Not long after the lovely aroma of 'chocolate mousse and cream puff' had wafted over the square, the hunger strike was called off.

Athens Airport

A new capital takes off

The old airport could handle 10 million complaints a year and employed state-of-the-art equipment to keep passengers waiting until their overbooked plane had secretly departed. How would the new Athens Airport fare?

In response to allegations of massive overstaffing, Olympic Airways have announced they are setting up a 3,000-member committee to investigate. Even with earmuffs, passengers flying with the state airline often complain about that deafening sound shortly before take-off when the captain asks the crew to fasten their seatbelts.

Why bash Olympic? Strikes, high fares, delays and a poor ground service to other airlines can be countered by at least a few dedicated employees, an exceptional safety record in the air – my religious friends might like to knock on wood at this point – and the prospect of privatisation which could dramatically improve their performance.

Not all problems can be blamed on OA. Travellers passing through Athens have had a raw deal over the years at the outgoing ('Hellenikon') airport where, in stark contrast to several charming island airports, there's usually a lack of seating, one miserable cafe, stray dogs, floods and a half-an-hour wait for a five-second bus ride to the plane 60 metres away. But the entertainment can't be beaten. In December 2000, a truck hit the Bulgarian president's plane (a Greek speciality – see Page 45). He wasn't on board. In October 1998, a dissident Ethiopian journalist 'tried to hijack an Olympic Airways jet while armed with an airline butter knife' (*Athens News*). Greece's humanity shone through here as it so often does in such situations. Not only was the hijacker allowed to surrender peacefully but I think a court let him stay in the country after doing 500 hours of community service in a sandwich bar.

Two years later came another bizarre incident when an executive at FAGE, the dairy products company, was late for his Athens-Brussels flight and phoned in a bomb threat, hoping this unoriginal ploy would hold up the plane. Rather than a bomb, I'd have thought a senior FAGE official would say, 'There's a strawberry yoghurt in the fridge', but apparently not. He was caught because his efficient secretary had put him through after first giving his name and position.

Back to the future. The $2 billion German-Greek Athens International Airport – officially called Eleftherios Venizelos which foreigners won't be able to handle – is scheduled to open as this book was *[Ed: meant to be]* going to press in March 2001. (Okay, I confess, the prime minister asked me to delay publication to avoid Greece having two major events in the same month.) Only a handful of trivial afterthoughts still need fixing, such as a main road connecting the airport to the capital, and all will be well. Civil aviation workers have campaigned for part of 'Hellenikon', in the south, to remain in use when the new facility opens at Spata in the east, insisting the planned park and an F-16 runway can exist side-by-side. If it's true that the Olympic archery event might be held at the old site, the transition needs to be swift or we could be seeing some very unusual plane crashes.

If any of the new operator's big boys are reading this, three important questions: 1) Have you made plans to regulate the taxi drivers at the airport, ie will you have their names and photos, union membership number and registration plates? 2) Will you be selling my books? 3) Will you have an effective and immediate disciplinary system in place so that when the complaints about one particular driver reach, say, the 100,000 mark, you will stop him ever coming to the airport again – in any cab? How long before a taxi driver takes a couple of unsuspecting Japanese tourists to classical Sparta 200km away in the Peloponnese rather than Spata, 20km from the centre of Athens?

Remember: Your two runways, bookshops, main passenger terminal, ISBN directories, security, author royalties, baggage handling, advance order service and personnel will undoubtedly be first class, and your radar reasonable, but if you can't control the taxi drivers, who rip off many Greeks as well as visitors, then even if you commercially succeed, you will fail – and fail big time.

True story time. At the old airport in August 1998, an admittedly naive Australian tourist paid 38,500 drachmas for a 13km ride to the city centre. In dollars (and euros) that's over 100 when the actual fare should have been less than 10, tip included. To be fair to the driver, he said he did not know the passenger had given him so much money. To be fair to the passenger, what a load of crap.

◪ Foreigners enjoy flying out of the capital because it's the only time they get to see where the actual streets are.

For a month I walked from the *Athens News* in Christou Lada Street to a friend's office in Kolonaki's Sina Street, wandering around scores of roads and squares and getting more and more lost. You try it.

At the end of Christou Lada, named after a justice minister who was assassinated there, cross Stadiou and find Eduardo Lo. At some point you need to go over the very busy Panepistimiou (aka Venizelou) and then start your search for Sina.

Each trip used to take me half an hour but any native Athenian will do it in 10 minutes tops. You see, the names change but the direction does not. In fact, from start to finish, you stay on exactly the same street.

Note: The new facility, which has been unfairly described, possibly by me, as the only airport in the world reachable by air, finally opened on 28 March 2001. After a chaotic start – when (German) management said that (Greek) baggage staff were trying to stuff oversized suitcases into sensitive computerised machinery – the airport is now operating smoothly. Often described as soulless, the facility is clinically efficient. Even taxi outrages have declined, partly thanks to an excellent 24-hour bus service. As of 1 December 2001, IAS (Integrated Airline Solutions) was the front runner to take control of Olympic but bankruptcy is not out of the question.

Athens News

Tales from the South Pacific

Now approaching 50, the Athens News has always informed, occasionally entertained and sometimes erred (if you count getting the date wrong). Through it all the paper has remained an important part of readers' lives.

Say hello to Pete.

Despite an impressive pre-lunch interview, cooperation between Pete (not his real name) and the *Athens News* abruptly ended when he fell out of a helicopter (sic) not long after. Blessed with a sunny outlook on life – Pete's giant-sized glass, it's fair to say, was at least half full – his proofreading mistakes were subtle but serious, along the lines of *Bosnian Slerbs vow vengeance* or the dateline *Maddddrid*.

The *Athens News* was founded in 1952 by the irrepressible Yannis Horn. He remained publisher for an astonishing 47 years until his death, aged 88, on 15 October 1999, though the paper has been part of the Lambrakis Research Foundation since 1993. Not one of life's big, or even medium, spenders, Mr Horn had an amazing gift for seeking out rich advertisers and poor journalists. Every word in this book indirectly owes its existence to his ferocious determination to keep the newspaper alive during difficult times.

Any serious appraisal of the *Athens News* begins with the sheer quality of the staff who have left the paper. This sounds ironic but isn't. We have consistently attracted the very best (and sometimes the very worst) in the field, many of whom have gone on to greater success. All along, the paper has been a fun place to work at and we're rightly known as the 'kindergarten' of the Lambrakis empire.

Ever reader-friendly, with unusual promotions like 'Learn French with the *Athens News*', the paper has always steered clear of offensive content. Filth like *Government's 5 + 5 Wage Offer gets Unions' P + Off response* only appears, as a rule, under my name.

Stories and headlines remain our bread and butter, such as *Teacher who ate student won't be freed*, in the US, and the sublime *Traffic banned in Grozny, violators will be shot*, from Tass' English-language service. During a spell at the sports desk, *Hit Man Hit Hard*, about boxer Thomas Hearns, was indeed published, unlike my title for another fighter, Herbie Hide, who had vowed to seek out and destroy his opponent in the ring *(You can Hide but you can't Herbie)*. In Greece itself, *Three die in row over lost cat* concerned an 87-year-old who thought neighbours had nicked his furry friend. He shot them dead, followed by himself, after which the animal returned home.

Headline mistakes by the *Athens News* include *Massages for March 25*, the national holiday in Greece for which political leaders traditionally issue *messages*, and (Jesse*) Jackson feasts for Haitian refugees.* Take out the 'e' in feasts and you'll see what we meant. That's not all. We've had pictures of a clock being turned back an hour with the text underneath saying the clocks were going forward, and I was the one who got the date wrong, putting Saturday not Sunday. Other highlights in our history apparently include a proofreader robbing a bank and the weather forecast remaining unchanged for four months.

That's still not all. Our issue number is allegedly way out though no one knows whether the paper has always been published six days a week (ie not Mondays). If it has, it's almost 2,000 too low. Numbers aside, I'm researching *The correction will go in tomorrow - A history of the Athens News*. All e-mails to biscuitbrian@hotmail.com from former staff will be acknowledged. *[The author regrets being unable to enter into any outstanding wage disputes.]*

Since 1993, we have been pampered with modern technology. Before then, we improvised, periodically touching up Imelda Marcos' fading chin with a deft round stroke of the pen. During the junta days, with pressure from the embassies keeping us in print (unlike most Greek papers), the *Athens News* courageously wound up the dictatorship no end. George Washington quotes on freedom were sprinkled throughout the edition which reported US Vice President Spiro Agnew's arrival in 1973. Accurate mention of recruited schoolchildren greeting Agnew at the airport landed Mr Horn in a sweltering summer jail. Malicious rumours that on being released he took the cell's only fridge home with him are baseless.

Complaints, mistakes, apologies...and hard work and an ability to laugh at ourselves. Avoiding political extremes or party ties, we offer unbiased reporting with a genuine desire to help visitors and foreign residents understand Greece more. After half a century in a volatile business, we've earned the most valuable accolade: Readers trust us.

◪ In the late 1950s, Reuters reported the BP dividend wrongly, causing millions of pounds to be lost or gained on a frantic London stock exchange.

According to a *Times* obituary (January 1996) of Alfred Geiringer, then head of Reuters business information services, a meeting of senior executives was immediately called, and a bloodbath expected. Instead, Geiringer observed that if the financial community depended so much on Reuters, 'We are clearly not charging enough.' Subscriptions were immediately raised by a third. 'No subscribers cancelled.'

The obituary brought back to mind the legendary *Athens News* front-page headline for our 4-5 April 1982 edition (price 20 drachmas) just as the UK was preparing to send out forces to the South Atlantic to fight Argentina. Underneath the 'hat' – a top line saying *Falklands crisis in full swing* – a string of capital letters revealed a sensational world exclusive: BRITISH NAVY SAILS OFF FOR SOUTH PACIFIC.

We kept the price as it was.

Note: The *Athens News* became a weekly on 16 March 2001 (price 500 drachmas) and now comes out every Friday. *Church on Sunday* retained its name and can be found on that most important of pages – 11 – or sometimes 9 (or 54).

Athens Metro

Very nice but why is it underground?

The capital began to get that sinking feeling in October 1997 when a kiosk, one of thousands serving Athenians' daily needs for water, cigarettes and pornographic magazines, suddenly disappeared.

Exclusive! Did a giant volcanic explosion, followed by a massive tidal wave, sink Santorini into the ground around 1500 BC, as archaeologists have long assumed, or did our Bronze Age buddies try to build a metro underneath the island?

With the collapse this week of part of Panepistimiou Street, involving the sensational disappearance of a kiosk and attributed to the Metro tunnelling (even the Americans can't be blamed for this one, though they should, of course, pay for the kiosk's replacement), fears have grown that there could be much worse to come. Workers near to the kiosk claim their office block is sloping dangerously and an awful lot of shops are holding 'falling down' sales. The state lottery stands to make a fortune by getting punters to bet on which building will disappear next.

'Don't panic' is the message from Attiko Metro, the French-led consortium responsible for building the underground, and they're surely in a better position to know than the rest of us. Besides, they're hardly inexperienced at their job, having in the past successfully constructed underground transportation systems in Pompeii, Krakatoa, Pisa and Montserrat. *(Note to company lawyers: I'm joking guys, okay?)*

Not helping matters, conspiracy theorists claim the Metro doesn't exist because no lorries have been seen carrying displaced earth from the ground. Such a fraud would require the active participation of thousands of people pretending to work each day, though I concede the example of Syntagma Post Office proves this isn't wholly impossible.

Less sensationally, it's been argued that the existing underground is perfectly satisfactory (it isn't) and that it has the advantage of not being underground for 90% of the route stretching from leafy

Kifissia in the north to the port of Piraeus in the south. Not only is this nicer for passengers but it has the added bonus that most of the surrounding streets, and kiosks, are still with us. They've got a point. And I personally fear the main legacy of building a tunnel underneath the capital will be a massive number of bank vault robberies in the decades ahead.

Mockery often disguises ignorance. When the Metro is finished, we will all be singing the consortium's praises because the facts of this modern technological miracle speak for themselves: The extension links 18 kilometres of underground track and tunnel to 21 new stations and 15,000 lawyers.

Right from the start, the Athens Metro has excited passions. No name I'm afraid but a fairly senior construction worker got so fed up with the tunnelling delays imposed by archaeologists that one day he said he stormed out of work, went to nearby Plaka, bought a cheap, tacky vase from one of the dozens of tourist shops, broke it in half, smeared dirt all over a fragment, returned to work and placed it in the official collecting skip. I'm sure it was weeded out by the experts but he looks forward to seeing it on display.

◪ And the result?

Clean, bright and impressively fast, the Metro is a joy to travel on, including the latest Dafni-Syntagma extension in November 2000. Another extension, effectively linking up with the new airport, will be finished by May 2004. For many Athenians lucky enough to live on the line, there has been a great improvement in the quality of life, providing they remember to jump out of the way when a train is coming. Seriously now, journey time to work for some people has been cut from an hour on a bad day to a guaranteed seven minutes. 'Long' short journeys are now short, not long.

Since the 700-billion-drachma Metro began operating on 28 January 2000, my impression is that the centre of Athens has got slightly better for motorists, offsetting the tendency in recent years for traffic flow to continue deteriorating. But closing at midnight in a country with a 4am rush hour at weekends is idiotic and finding a place to park can be close to impossible at some stations.

Inside the Metro itself, the marble hasn't been splattered with graffiti, the seats on the trains are very comfortable with a nice bendy bit in the back and there will be air-conditioning by summer 2002, according to the operator.

But much more needs to be done with the capital's traffic.

First, stop crawling to foreign visitors. Don't automatically close all major roads if the twin brother of the second cousin of the deputy undersecretary in the Bulgarian sports department pops in to have his teeth checked.

Second, ban taxis. Inner-city circulation improves enormously whenever they're on strike.

Lastly, but most importantly, the pseudo-worship of democracy allows the entire centre to be regularly disrupted by as few as 200 protesters. At some point, demonstrators will try to block Metro stations. We should anticipate the problem and build them their own tunnel where they can shout as much as they like.

Curiously, only the fascists aren't allowed to take over the streets. They'd have a problem anyway. In January 2000, members of Golden Dawn, an extreme right-wing group, gathered around the statue of independence hero Kolokotronis sitting proudly on his horse, near Syntagma Square, and to say they were outnumbered by riot police would be seriously misleading. They were outnumbered by kiosk owners, outnumbered by trolley drivers, outnumbered by the homeless wanting 100 drachmas for a packet of tissues, outnumbered by teenagers busily chatting on mobile phones. At one point, they were almost outnumbered by the horse.

Note: Following the discovery in November 1998 that old tombstones had been (accidentally) used for marble paving around the entrance to the Syntagma station, an extra statement was added onto Greek donor cards: 'In the event of my death, I do/do not [delete as applicable] want my tombstone to be used in the building of the Athens Metro.'

Piraeus

We're not in Athens

When the 34-year-old 'Express Samina' went down off Paros on the night of 26 September 2000, killing 80, a grieving nation demanded answers to the Cycladic catastrophe. They soon wished they hadn't asked.

How dare the media discuss the idiotic claim that the 'Express Samina' was deliberately sunk for the insurance money?

Apart from such talk being incredibly tasteless, why don't people accept the far more obvious and mundane explanation for Tuesday night's accident, namely that: 1) The captain was reportedly asleep in bed. 2) The first mate was apparently chatting up a female passenger. 3) A trainee was allegedly steering the vessel at full-speed into well-known and easily visible rocks. 4) The rest of the crew, according to passengers, were watching the live Panathinaikos-Hamburg soccer match, which Panathinaikos won 1-0. 5) Those lifeboats which could be released were full of toilet rolls.

When an ancient Greek ship was found in July 1994 with around 800 5th century BC wine jugs on board, we could all guess why it went down. The truth is often very simple. That of course doesn't make it acceptable. Sadly, even if all five of the above claims are proven correct, there will probably be little long-term pressure for proper punishment even though the captain and first mate are effectively facing murder (or aggravated manslaughter) charges. It sounds flippant but the catastrophe's biggest legacy, apart from getting rid of dangerously old ships, could be to see crew banned from watching TV on board.

There were endless reports of undoubted acts of heroism by the fishermen of Paros and Greek conscripts, and not so many by the crew – eight of whom died and dead men can't defend themselves. Greek seamen have an excellent record in coming to the rescue of other vessels, and in the very worst of conditions.

You can gauge the gravity of a story by the degree to which Greek papers don't criticise foreign media coverage and so far I haven't heard any complaints. Indeed, the US State Department travel advisory telling Americans to avoid trips on the day of the forthcoming Greece-England World Cup match caused not a murmur of protest.

New Democracy leader Costas Karamanlis got it exactly right when he asked, 'Doesn't anyone have the decency to resign?' If the shipping minister held back the only working search & rescue helicopter for his own trip to the island, as alleged, he should resign. If the crews for the other defence ministry choppers hadn't been trained, the defence minister should resign. If they weren't trained because there wasn't enough money, the finance minister should resign. And if the media knew all about this but didn't say anything, I should resign.

Will anyone resign? See you next week.

◪ Timing is everything. This book was due to be released in summer 2000. The original introduction, which explains this chapter's remaining subtitle, was the following: 'By far the biggest success story in modern Greek history, and with money to buy out next door's capital a hundred times over, the proud people of Piraeus rarely boast about their nautical achievements. They don't need to. Just one thing: Don't call them Athenians.'

Hardly original but true nonetheless. Barely 10km away, the sea-propelled city detests being seen as a simple extension of capital pond life. Piraeus-based operators have made Greece a world power in the maritime industry with their oil-bearing fleets of VLCCs (Very Large Crude Carriers) and ULCCs (Ultra Large Crude Carriers). There are no FLCCs. Greece doesn't rank as high in any other area except tourism and tax evasion, where shipping is considered to have made a massive contribution as well.

Note: Just before midday, on Wednesday 29 November 2000, 64 days after the disaster, Pantelis Sfinias, the forceful managing director of Minoan (now Hellas) Flying Dolphins, which operated the 'Express Samina', jumped to his death from his sixth-floor seafront office after drinking heavily, according to the coroner's report. He was 62. No note was left. Two months later, in an open letter to Greece's shipping minister, seven British survivors blasted the evacuation procedures and said the death toll 'could have been far, far lower'. The ship was just three nautical miles from harbour and the sea warm. The report into the disaster is believed to blame the crew for failing to close watertight doors and thereby limiting the effects of the flooding from a small three-by-one-metre gash in the vessel. The captain and first mate remained in jail, end of September 2001, partly for their own safety.

CHAPTER TWO

The Unforgettable Greece

Everyone's got their own special list of things to remember. Here's mine.

People Power

Best thing about Greece? Greeks

The Greek character always shines in emergencies. As then premier Andreas Papandreou fought for his life in December 1995, this touching snapshot of kindness developed amidst the media scrum.

It was nice to see.

At a press conference on the now famous seventh floor of the Onassis Heart Centre, photographers jostled to get the best shot of medical spokesman Prof. Grigoris Skalkeas giving the latest news on the condition of Prime Minister Andreas Papandreou.

As Skalkeas started speaking, his words broadcast live on almost every TV & radio station in the country, a young, thin man clambered onto a shaky table and began taking 'aerial' shots. Nearby, a fairly elderly, very large and extremely tired photographer, his view totally blocked by other colleagues, glanced at the table and weighed up his one in a hundred million chances of doing the same. Then he simply tapped the leg of the guy on the table and gave him his camera. The sky-high photographer not only took it but spent a couple of valuable minutes getting quality photos from various angles. Same paper? Unlikely. Friends? Possible. More likely, illness – maybe death – brings out the best in all of us.

There's been much talk about a night-time vigil outside Athens' Syngrou Avenue hospital with 'hundreds there for Andreas' as millions of fans and his controversial third wife Dimitra Liani call him. When I went at 3am there wasn't *one* there for Andreas. But now there really are hundreds, if not thousands, of loyal followers, fearing the worst.

Even the right-wing are keeping quiet, though they've long despised him. Unlike zillions of other claimants, Papandreou *was* the founder of Pasok, the most successful post-dictatorship political party. For good or for bad – and some of it was really good – Andreas is credited with changing the way Greeks felt about themselves and their relation to the outside world, smashing a seemingly unbreakable hold on the country by a right-wing clique bordering on lunacy and replacing it with, at times, an equally unwelcome nationalism-fired and personality-driven quasi-socialism. One of Papandreou's major achievements as prime minister for most of the 1980s was to keep Greece in the European Community, as it was, despite calls, mostly by himself, to leave.

You can gauge a nationality by the attitude towards death and illness. When leading personalities are seriously sick, papers often voluntarily withhold information. Cancer is rarely referred to by name, rather the (inaccurate) 'incurable disease'. The Greek media at the centre are quiet and respectful, with the exception of the 'no smoking' rule.

I found myself intrigued by world heart specialist Magdi Yacoub, flown in specially, saying Papandreou had '*a* hope', pronouncing the 'a' as in 'day' rather than the slightly more common 'uh'. The significance of this, I concluded, reflected more on my own mental health than Papandreou's physical condition.

But have no doubt: These are desperately difficult days for the 76-year-old Andreas. The kidneys are poor, heart as bad as before, his lungs – well they're in real trouble and all asthmatics out there will be willing him on in his battle to breathe as he fights permanent exhaustion. The political icon and ruthless operator, who in his prime beat everyone with little effort, now has one simple, unambiguous wish: To lay down his head and get some rest.

Andreas Papandreou was replaced by Costas Simitis on 18 January 1996. Looking appallingly weak, Papandreou bravely left the hospital on 21 March and died at home in Ekali, northern Athens, three months later on 23 June 1996. Simitis remains prime minister as of 1 December 2001, having won two general elections, the last an all-night cliffhanger with just 1.1% finally separating the top two parties. For once, Church on Sunday was almost wrong:

Sunday 9 April 2000 It will be a landslide in today's general election. For ruling party Pasok and, above all, for Premier Costas Simitis.

Even the nature of the campaign, deeply restrained by Greek standards, has reflected the Simitis era in which shouting slogans and exciting the masses has given way to actually doing something. Can anyone deny that his governments, modest but effective, have put Greece in the strongest position, economically, diplomatically, even militarily, in living memory? Thanks to Simitis, to succeed in the future, parties will need to detoxify their nationalism and come up with honest answers to problems which directly impact ordinary people's lives, such as the shrinking Communist Party's pledge to withdraw from Nato.

When Pasok, led by Simitis, won the 22 September 1996 election, I was sub-editing the front page of the *Athens News*. You might remember sensitive headlines like *Missing Ben: Is he dead or was he sold?* For our main title after that election, we eventually came up with *Simitis starts quiet revolution.*

Four years later it's still quiet. And it remains a revolution.

Sunday 16 April 2000 The final results from the 2000 general election (with my forecasts last week in brackets) were: Pasok 158 seats (181), New Democracy 125 (95), KKE 11 (12), Coalition of the Left 6 (4) and Thicki 0 (8).

I stand by my predictions which were accurate within a margin of error of 900%.

◪ The people will always talk about Papandreou but history will remember Simitis. Several other politicians have stood in their shade over the past 10 years.

In March 2001, Dimitris Avramopoulos, PR genius and rumoured mayor of Athens, started a crypto-party under the characteristically banal name, Free Citizens' Movement (KEP). Don't underestimate this guy. There's a terrible chance he could be ruining *[Ed: Not 'running'?]* Greece in the not-terribly-distant future. Seven months later, Stephanos Manos, creator and leader of the Liberal Party, by far the most advanced, progressive, tolerant, forward-thinking, daring, capable and sensible party in Greece, announced the Liberals were calling it a day because no one supported them.

In July 1999, Foreign Minister George Papandreou, son of Andreas and grandson of George, the 1960s prime minister, astonished everyone. He declared that what the minority in Thrace called themselves – ethnic Turks, as most prefer; Greek Muslims, as state propaganda christens them; or Icelandic Methodists, my suggested compromise – paled in importance alongside the need to keep borders unchanged and the area stable. Such remarks shattered

No. 3 in the pantheon of taboo subjects in Greece – the other two I'm afraid I can't tell you – and Papandreou was absolutely right. He could be a great premier himself one day soon and has already helped Greece put a traditionally cold Turkey in the microwave *[Ed: Do you mean relations have warmed?]*.

Momentarily infamous was Gerasimos Yiakoumatos, the talkative conservative MP whose house was burgled in a crime wave which led to an anti-Albanian frenzy. An enraged Yiakoumatos gave this pledge: 'If anything happens to my family, I will shoot [then Public Order Minister George] Romeos right in the face.' After widespread condemnation, the deputy insisted his remarks had been *misinterpreted*. Maybe he meant 'right in the face but a little bit to the left.'

Intermittent cabinet minister Theodoros Pangalos stands out for his wit, courage, competence and a classic putdown of an excited presenter at the start of a TV interview: 'I'm sorry. Who am I talking to?' In October 2000, Pangalos was in tears at a street-naming ceremony in Cyprus for alternate Greek foreign minister, the Cypriot Yiannos Kranidiotis, who had died a year before in a bizarre accident whilst flying to Romania. 'It is hard to see your friend turn into a road,' said Pangalos. The English translation adds unintentional levity to a strikingly poignant observation.

Politicians often speak in unusual places. Defence Minister Akis Tsochadzopoulos once discussed (unclassified) aspects of national security at a nightclub in front of a gleaming drum kit. Sadly, a CNN programme on Greek-Turkish relations failed to show the Tsochadzopoulos clip because a researcher thought it was part of the Dusty Springfield obit.

Food for Thought

Religion, identity and yoghurt

In December 1998, Greek society was rocked by unbelievable news. One headline said it all: THEY THREW YOGHURT! And, worse, they had chucked it at the most popular person in Greece.

It happened at noon on a Monday.

Archbishop Christodoulos, the country's spiritual leader, was greeting his flock in Aegio, north Peloponnese, when from nowhere a yoghurt was tossed in his direction. Christodoulos, with his above-average-sized hat, was an easy target but the yoghurt thankfully landed on the pavement, splattering an old man's back.

As police searched a nearby building, rumours of an assassination attempt grew. Detectives are currently investigating if yoghurt plays a significant role in the liturgy of any non-Orthodox group based in Greece.

Many questions remain unanswered: What flavour was the yoghurt, fruit or plain? Was it cow's milk or goat's milk? Who made it? Will the cow/goat testify? Where was it bought? Greenpeace want to know if the pot can be recycled. Ominously, one eyewitness claimed to have seen a *second* yoghurt thrown. Experts said the 'splatter pattern' indicated this wasn't the act of a lone madman.

Four days later and another yoghurt attack, this time in Athens on the mayor of Peristeri. Political analysts are now warning that *Yoghurtgate* could start an uncontrollable grassroots tradition whereby famous people automatically have yoghurt thrown at them whenever they leave the centre of Athens, the flavour to be determined by a local referendum ahead of their visit.

While sociologists agonised over whether TV cookery shows had influenced the assailants, it was tantalisingly suggested that the whole incident in Aegio might have been caused by a simple misunderstanding. The archbishop was there 24 hours after the St Nicholas name day celebrations. The Greek word for festival/celebration is similar to yoghurt and it's possible that a few locals might have got confused.

One thing is clear. The telegenic Christodoulos (see *Men in black*, Page 103) has been slammed in the media for his 'excessive' nationalism – he says he's proud to be Greek – but he still commands widespread public support. Indeed, a poll of married Greek males revealed him to be the most admired person in the country after the man who threw his mother-in-law out of the house for eating his dinner.

And you have to give Christodoulos credit for the way he down-played the 'isolated incident'.

Others were much more worried. Well-known yoghurt maker FAGE immediately distanced themselves from the attack and announced they will no longer be putting *Throw-by* dates on their products.

Even more dramatically, a pressure group hitherto considered the most powerful organisation in Greece was forced onto the defensive. A spokesman for the yoghurt division of the National Trifle Association insisted that 'Yoghurts don't hurt people, people hurt people'. Despite such claims, immediate calls were made in parlia-ment for stricter yoghurt-licensing laws to require under-18s and adults with a good aim to wait a week before purchase.

Cool, calm and collected, the archbishop left the next day for Paris where street vendors reported an unseasonal increase in the sale of croissants.

Note: a) Wanting to walk in the footsteps of St Paul, Pope John Paul II came to Athens 4-5 May 2001, his first visit to Greece. Frail but characteristically courageous, JP's brief ecumenical cuddle initially aroused furious opposition in this overwhelmingly Orthodox country. Uniquely, the Old Calendarists even disagreed over the actual date of his visit. Thankfully, the pope charmed the rosaries off his hosts and graciously apologised for past Catholic sins against the Orthodox Church. Amidst millions of daft conspiracy theories at the time of the visit, some going as far back as the Great Schism of 1054, the best was that the Jews (sic) had invited the pope to Athens in order to hurt Greece's reputation abroad. b) The very first *Church on Sunday* (31 October 1993) praised the 'highly original way' of guaranteeing increased attendance at Attica Cathedral in Kifissia, northern Athens, where 'rival camps of supporters – claiming their bishop was the rightful one to conduct services – fought each other in full view of the cameras'. When one of the protagonists passed away, I cried for hours before wondering who would conduct the funeral and making plans to book my seat.

◪ *Wednesday 21 June 2000* To a Syntagma Square packed with the deeply devout and the equally deeply disturbed, Archbishop Christodoulos gave one of the grimmest warnings heard in recent times as the ID card crisis reached its peak.

Christodoulos predicted that if star signs *[Ed: Mr Church means religious affiliation]* were taken off identity cards, the cabinet would then press ahead with removing the cross from the Greek flag, taking religion out of schools and closing all McDonald's. *[Ed: Are you sure?]*

There was huge disagreement over the number of demonstrators. One kiosk owner estimated a whopping 800,000. The wire services went for 120,000, which just goes to show that journalists and kiosk owners don't always agree. For what it's worth, I stopped counting at 14.

The Church's proposed solution is to hold a referendum on the issue. Unfortunately, we'd end up voting non-stop since everyone would want one, such as that burning cause, the Association of Friends of Cremation, whose meetings must be a bundle of laughs. Sources tell me that in any referendum to make cremation legal, those against would vote NO while those in favour would set fire to the ballot box.

Is a compromise out there somewhere? The government insists that EU law forbids religious affiliation on ID cards to avoid any potential discrimination. Okay, instead of stating your religion, why not state your uncle's? If the cabinet wants to be devious, it will offer a single referendum with two questions – one on the ID cards and the other on whether Andreas Papandreou's long-abandoned plan for the Church to give up some of its massive landholdings should be revived.

I suspect the ID controversy would end rather quickly.

Note: The decree formally removing religious affiliation from identity cards was officially published on 17 July 2000. The Church's petition drive began in September that year. An impressive, albeit unverified, total of 3,008,901 signatures was announced by the Church at the end of August 2001, out of a population of around 10 million Orthodox – or 1,405 more than Pasok's (verified) 2000 election vote. The archbishop remains popular with the ignorant masses *[Ed: I think we better change this]* but his extreme nationalism has been ridiculed by those true patriots not obsessed with forever being on the telly *[Ed: And this]*. In one outburst, Christodoulos blamed the Jews (sic) for the ID crisis. The issue was brought to a merciful halt by President Costis Stephanopoulos who refused Christodoulos' request to back a referendum on the issue. A law allowing for a crematorium (possibly for non-Orthodox only) has been promised by the government. Alain Delon has not commented on either issue.

A Fright at the Theatre

Final curtain comes down on one critic

During 1994-95 I reviewed several plays by English-language amateur theatre groups but bowed out gracefully after upsetting too many people. Why? Judge for yourself in this 7 February 1995 review, reprinted word for word.

'Arse' and 'Bastard' within the first 10 seconds of the Little Theatre Company's weekend double-bill got it off to a fine start from which it never really recovered.

The acting was reasonable enough but John Flynn's non-expletive writing weak and unoriginal in both *Time is Money* and *That's What I Told Your Father.*

The *Time is Money* script seemed a little Anglocentric at times. Panayiotis (Andreas Voutopoulos) asks Yiorgos (the impressively dishevelled Richard Calkin) if he remembered the war or, as the script puts it, 'Do you remember the war?' Yiorgos asks which one ('Which one?'), to which Panayiotis exclaims which one ('Which one!!!') and, well, to cut a long story short, the answer is the one between Germany and Britain ('The one between,' sorry). But surely some mention could have been made of the Greece-Italy tie along with the Civil War.

As the two men reminisce about what they would have liked to do in life if given another chance – and if you know which war hadn't come – light relief is given from the manic Carrie Gerolimpou (playing the *Ouzeri Woman* – John has a knack for descriptions). Her unbelievable bottom wiggle, whilst wiping a table, will certainly be remembered long after the applause has started.

The title, by the way, comes from the very last remark of the production, which is a nice way of reminding you which play you've just been watching – though not necessarily why. I got the feeling that had the English woman (played with great annoyance by Kerry Dolman) called after the hurriedly departing duo, 'And don't scratch the sideboard – I've just bought it!', we would be seeing 'The Little Theatre Company presents *That's What I Told Your Father* plus *And Don't Scratch the Sideboard – I've Just Bought It!*'

Kerrie [my inconsistent spelling], by the way, wanted her chairs mended and knives sharpened. And that was the complicated part of the plot.

The second play started off with a Sinatra song in total darkness – which has huge potential for my HAMS friends [see below].

Eleni Nikolina played Suzanne Carlisle well, giving out the freshness and enthusiasm of a young woman about to get married. And given a better script, her exchanges with Grandmother Christine (played by Jennifer Couroucli) could have really taken off. Playing the star actress Magda Carlisle, Angela Makri was reasonable enough. When she had to ring her ex-husband for the first time after many years, you shared in her real discomfort. June Maxwell was the comfortably irritating secretary, Izzy.

The plot dealt with Suzanne wanting to know about her real father. Her mother eventually tells her she was raped. Dealing with such an emotive subject is difficult at the best of times but, in this context, it was as inadvisable as the famed British comedy team doing a *Carry On Holocaust!*

The programme notes to these two short (30-minute) plays read like a legal disclaimer. Making rightful mention of Flynn's talents as a painter, the only reference to his writing is, 'John Flynn has written the plays you will be seeing tonight,' and, a few lines on, 'John paints in the morning and, in the evening, writes. He started writing plays.......John was born in Chicago.'

The seven dots are almost as if something was going to be added – deep intensity, visionary scribe, etc – but in the end no one could think of anything to say. Filling the page was clearly an ordeal since the programme goes on to tell us that John 'lives on the ground floor of a house in Pangrati, has a garden, several cats and a view of the sea which, on clear days, brings him the blue hills of Aegina (sic)'.

Attendance was appalling – late 20s the evening I was there which is unforgivable, especially for a charming (Modern Times) theatre in Ambelokipi [central-ish Athens]. People don't want to travel but English theatre should always be supported. This review is my contribution. Those there enjoyed it.

In conclusion, the pen might well be mightier than the sword – but not John's.

◪ I will always have a soft spot for the Little Theatre Company, especially John Flynn, since there wasn't a single complaint when the above review was published. Now that's what I call style.

Fairly or fairly, HAMS, the Hellenic Atrocious Musical Society, have suffered the most over the years, including my deeply malicious claim that their Christmas medley had been condemned by Amnesty International. Throw-away comments in the dedication of my last book might also have confused some readers so, just for the record, HAMS are *not* the musical wing of HAMAS (and the A, of course, stands for Amateur). What they are is a big-hearted group who have always welcomed me back to their performances and I salute them all.

Throughout my reviews, Editor Romolo Gandolfo, despite his dawning realisation that we were upsetting a significant portion of our readership, simply encouraged me to mention anything positive. Thus one review of a frightening performance by HAMS praised the 'excellent refreshments'. This brought the inevitable letter of complaint from an understandably anonymous 'HAMS fan': 'If Mr Church had spent less time sampling the "excellent" refreshments and paid more attention to the actual show...'

Greek Police

Red trousers at night, copper's delight

Greece is a paradise for columnists. Something is always happening. In April 1998, the country was in the middle of a crime scare and the police had gone a-huntin'...

Returning home at four o'clock early Saturday morning, today's column was beginning to worry me. As you can see, the pressure of coming up with original material every Sunday burdens my entire week. Was it too early to urge readers to start sending in their summer postcards?

Suddenly I heard a car driving at great speed along a road which I had just walked past. Coming into my street, the same vehicle seemed to be getting closer and faster. As I descended the steps leading to the entrance of my block of flats, the car screeched to a halt right outside and some words were shouted in my direction.

I turned and, despite being slightly tipsy, realised that it was a police car. If I understood correctly, the next words were 'Come here' and 'Put your hands up'.

There were two cops, one of whom was perched behind his open door on the far side from me. His arms and legs were stretched out in action mode but whether he'd drawn his gun (which all Greek policemen carry) I don't know. They seemed tense, possibly because I had momentarily before put my hand inside my pocket to get the apartment keys.

Now the police here, routinely ignored by most Greeks, are unpredictable. Many journalists will remember with affection their fantastic outdoor demonstration of emergency road traps a few years back. TV cameras were invited to see cars forcibly stopped at high speed, drivers ordered out, searched, a helicopter hovering above, it all looked amazingly genuine. Only gradually did you realise it *was* and that these were innocent members of the public being randomly stopped and humiliated. It's so refreshing to live in a spin-less country where some senior police official actually thought this would get good publicity. It didn't, the press killed them (just as they did when invited along to watch riot police attack a Gypsy camp).

With this and 1,001 other crime stories in mind, I walked slowly back up the steps to the street and muttered in Greek that I was English, unable to recall the Greek for 'I'm not Albanian', the nationality automatically, often wrongly, blamed for crime. As the brain started functioning again (okay, I had drunk a lot), I quickly added that I worked for the Lambrakis media colossus.

Still suspicious, they asked me to put my hands on top of the police car in classic TV-style and the nicer one on my side of the pavement frisked me – though only at the top – after which my hands were allowed down. Having repeated I didn't speak much Greek, the good cop asked:

Do you speak English?
Yes I do.
Where have you come from?
From Amfitheas Avenue. I came by taxi from Athens, from the Lambrakis *organismos*, 3 Christou Lada. I'm a journalist.

'My' bilingual policeman visibly relaxed and explained that someone wearing red trousers, which I was, had just broken into a local supermarket. Surprisingly, and impressively, the same cop apologised. I insisted on showing him a press card and they drove off.

Whether or not the red trousers were a simple excuse to stop someone, I won't be wearing them again. They're in the wash anyway.

Advice for people stopped by the police? Don't run, do as they say and answer their questions. All this naturally assumes that you haven't raided the nearest supermarket. Sadly, but probably true, nationality (English) and colour (snow pink) were also on my side.

How bad it could have been is not worth thinking about. This coming Wednesday, by sheer coincidence, the subject of my *Learn Greek in 25 Years* weekly lesson is cereal packets and what words we can learn from the back of them. I have been collecting and buying such boxes for the past few weeks.

If I had been carrying a bag, they would definitely have opened it. Picture the scene: Hands still on the car. I keep claiming to be a respectable journalist for Greece's biggest media organisation, hardly the kind of guy to break into the local supermarket. Crowds gather as the policemen open the bag.

And what do they find? Newspapers, documents, a mini-cassette recorder perhaps? No. A packet of Frosties and some unfinished Cornflakes.

◪ Following on from last week's column, I have received a fax from Aleks, an Albanian living in Crete, kindly telling me the Greek for 'I'm not Albanian'.

I was so touched and humbled by the letter writer's humility that I suggested to the Editor we lead the next day with *Albanian nicks fax machine*. But the *Athens News* always gives people the benefit of the doubt unless we're short of stories.

[In a later letter] Aleks says he speaks German, Greek, English, French and 'my Albanian is far better than yours'. I don't have an Albanian, Aleks, but I take your word for it.

Note: a) The police are very proud of their 613.8-million-drachma computerised fingerprint-matching machine. Although there were a few predictable glitches on the first day, when the man operating the machine was arrested and charged with 786,931 separate offences, it is now playing a crucial role in the fight against crime. b) In July 1999 an armed drug addict entered a bank in Kypseli, central Athens, and demanded all of 1,000 drachmas (around $3). He was arrested by passing police. Later that year, in December, the director of ONISILOS, Greece's association of former convicts, was sadly murdered by a departing member. c) A mysterious skeleton, feet encased in concrete, was found up north in September 2001. The manner of death suggested a mob hit but *Church on Sunday* wonders if it could have been suicide: A builder with financial problems, maybe? There was talk of comparing a DNA sample of the skeleton with that of a missing associate of infamous hitman Carlos the Jackal. Here's another idea: Why not DNA the suspected victim's patio and see if the concrete matches? I have yet to find out what kind of cement was used – Blue Circle Mastercrete or Gray Portland Lime – and while understandably this issue might not matter to grieving relatives, it is certainly of interest to those of us thinking of carrying out some minor home improvements.

Earthquakes

How to predict them after they've happened

August 1999: 17,000 die in Turkey. September 1999: 143 are killed in Greece. October 1999: Greek seismologists (wrongly) forecast another Big One. It was time for a real man to stand up and tell the public to stop panicking.

Athenians who flee the capital this weekend out of fear of another major earthquake should be thoroughly ashamed of themselves, *writes Brian Church from Lesvos.*

It's very embarrassing. My sister planned her holiday on this lovely Aegean island six months ago, honestly, yet with all the vague and irresponsible speculation about the 45-second 8.2 quake at 3.17 this afternoon, all my friends think I've done a runner.

But it's not just me out of town I can tell you. I don't buy the Editor's note on the front of this paper: *We apologise for today's four-page edition which is due to technical problems caused by the printer's hangover.* They've all fled, the cowards.

If there really is a whopper this weekend, two things are certain. First, everyone will want to buy shares in VAN, the controversial earthquake school which specialises in predicting quakes after they've happened, according to their critics, with a success rate of 85%. For admirers determined to stand by their VAN, they're the only serious, independent research group. And more to the current point, they're predicting an imminent quake. A biggie. This weekend. Hence an emptying Athens.

The second definite consequence of a temblor in the capital is that I will be okay because I'm in Lesvos, ha! ha! ha! (I can see all the world headlines now: LESVOS FLATTENED. Should I perish, no flowers or donations to charity, please. Instead every mourner must bear a copy of my *Learn Greek in 25 Years* book, still on sale in Eleftheroudakis and Compendium.)

It's a natural human reaction to make light of what scares us – and when people are buried alive in collapsed buildings, everyone's scared. Going to bed not sure if you will be violently shaken awake or flattened by the floors above you is deeply unsettling. Like most

Athenians, I guess, I stared at my ceiling for a long while. Very few of us have been able to completely relax since 2.56 on that Tuesday afternoon, 7 September 1999, when the 5.9 Richter earthquake struck, its epicentre a mere 20 kilometres (12.5 miles) north of central Athens.

Up until then it had been a quiet week. All Monday had to offer was the Orthodox Church's Holy Synod laying down the conditions for a papal visit to Greece (see Note a), Page 28). John Paul II could come if he showed 'humility and penitence' and ran the 800 metres in less than two minutes. Analysts saw it as an historic overture to the Roman Catholics. Besides, the Synod did agree that he could visit as a head of state and latest reports from the Vatican say the pope, genuinely keen to encourage Christian unity at the dawn of a new millennium, is in training.

And then.

Wobble, wobble, wobble is the best I can describe it. Like ice skating in the dark after seven beers with a ferret down your trousers. Telephone lines were immediately put out of order and (every cloud has a silver living) mobile phones too. The biggest headache for foreigners was how to stop our families overseas from worrying. Only my teenage nephew seemed unperturbed, asking in an e-mail: 'Did it hit ya flat?' My mum was in tears on hearing that I was alive. I think I've phrased that wrongly.

No doubt loads of you think I'm so vain that my first post-quake action was to ring up the stores and check that my books were okay. But let's end on a serious note, a rarity for this column. Don't worry, major quakes are truly rare, it's over, and our task now is to do whatever we can to help the survivors.

Sleep well.

Note: A quake measuring 5.7 on the Richter scale and 'We're all gonna die!' in the Church household rocked Skyros, in the Aegean, on 26 July 2001. Athens was well wobbled in the process. No deaths, minor damage. Likewise on 14 November 2001, my name day, 4.5R.

CHAPTER THREE

The War of Words & The Words of War

Principles. Passion.
Politics. Problems.
And the Eurovision Song Contest.

The Balkans

Where are they?

If a taxi driver asks me how my mother's doing, I automatically look at the meter. If he asks me what I think of the Balkans, I automatically switch the subject.

It's a very clever strategy. Get Greece and Turkey together by agreeing in advance to discuss only the little things and then hope the developing trust and friendship will make it easier to approach much bigger issues.

So in July 1999 the two crosstown rivals met to talk about double taxation, cultural exchanges, tourism and other raging controversies. I hope it works though I wouldn't be surprised if, in 2035, Turkey and Greece get very close to an agreement on Cyprus only for the whole deal to be wrecked by a simmering dispute over DVD import licenses.

Catchy intro aside, the Cyprus dispute is no laughing matter, even with the recognised republic's move towards EU membership, and the pressure this puts on the Turkish-Cypriot side to join in. More to the point, what's all this got to do with the Balkans?

I've got skilled at changing the subject, you see, the only time in my life I've tried hard to avoid getting into arguments, especially during the cumulative Balkan tragedies throughout the 1990s. Some Serbs were unamused to discover that their leader, arch thug Slobodan Milosevic, was somehow more popular in Greece than in Yugoslavia itself.

Milosevic had very few real friends here but the 1999 Nato bombing of Serbia, after countless atrocities by Slobo and Co., caused hysteria in Greece. It was a nation close to going mad. Maybe justifiably mad, but still mad. Almost every person in the country was seriously upset and the crisis the sole subject of conversation.

Looking back, whatever you think of the now beautifully incarcerated Milosevic, he clearly had far more of a role in the wars' estimated 200,000 deaths (along with other ultra-nationalist despots like Croatia's Tudjman) than, say, my Aunty Gladys.

A more mature response, mixed with real fears of a mass wave of refugees, was seen in Greece with the turmoil in the neighbouring Former Yugoslav Republic of Macedonia (FYROM) in 2001. A Skopje government amnesty was clinched in return for the ethnic Albanian guerrillas handing over their weapons to Nato peacekeepers (the rebels proceeded to surrender 3,400 rifles, 150 mobile rocket launchers and two Tolis Voskopoulos CDs).

Through all the fiascos, flare-ups and flashpoints, some here have remained convinced that the world's leading papers are part of one colossal anti-Hellenic conspiracy, though I guess more than a few Turks also think their country is treated unfairly.

The *New York Times* is such an able publication that its staff can be paid by both Greek and Turkish agents – and the Israelis, obviously – and still be against both Greece and Turkey, depending on your viewpoint.

When the *Washington Post* published a critical article about Greece's security for the 2004 Games on the same day that the IOC's Jacques Rogge was due to visit Athens, out went the media message to be readily adopted by millions: This is deliberate sabotage. Not sloppy writing or unsubstantiated claims or fair comment but sabotage. Real journalists – both Greek and foreign – recognised an inspection visit by the IOC was the breathtakingly obvious time to print an article on the Athens Olympic Games as opposed to waiting until the Ugandan foreign minister travelled to Syria for bilateral trade talks.

The political hallmark of the 1990s in Greece was an abandonment of ideological belief by mostly left-wingers and the simultaneous mass adoption of ultra-nationalism in its place, often fuelled by resentment, boredom, laziness and lunacy.

Some nuts have had a kernel of truth. A large number of inexperienced (and greedy) small investors lost considerable sums of money on Sofokleous Street and big fish might well have manipulated the Athens Stock Exchange. But at the same time the workings of a capitalist bourse have been misunderstood: There are winners because there are losers. The money you gain is often the money somebody else loses.

For good or for bad – this misguided English liberal, possibly MI6, obviously thinks bad – Greece has been the only country in Europe where you can get opinion polls showing 99.9% of respondents against something, such as the Nato bombing of Serbia, though the Chechens can get stuffed. It's never easy finding yourself a vocal member of the 0.1% community – itself, true Greek-style, split into several factions – and a greater diversity of viewpoints (or at least more than one) is needed in some areas.

However, moderation is far stronger these days and we are thankfully light years away from the Macedonian madness in the early 1990s which included Greece boycotting a Holocaust remembrance ceremony because of the name dispute with FYROM (sic). Sensitive subjects like Athens lacking a proper mosque and the treatment of conscientious objectors (or British plane-spotters) are also being examined and slowly rectified.

The country is clearly moving forward.

But here's a fear: Will the lack of an 'automatic' and predictable way of thinking, and the absence of nationalist propaganda from the cradle to the grave, damage the bonds which make this country so united (and frankly lovable), causing uncertainty, unrest and chaos, and leading to discord, crime and even the effective breakup of society?

That's putting it very simplistically but then I am very simple. And what do I know anyway? As one anonymous but highly perceptive comment in an *Athens News* reader survey put it: 'The idiot who writes as Brian Church is not a journalist.'

And let me end on an even humbler note. An apology no less. I would like to sincerely apologise to anyone I've unintentionally upset over the years through my column or in this book, especially those confused ethnic half-halfs, expat extremists and ultra-nationalist bigots who have so seriously damaged this country over the years. Your time has come. Your time has gone. Goodbye. *[Ed: That's an apology?]*

◪ DW Brogan's *The American Problem* (Hamish Hamilton, 1944) recounts the 1820s story about a man seized by a mob which has reason to doubt his loyalty to the popular Monroe Doctrine.

Fighting for his life, the guy starts shouting: 'I didn't say I was AGAINST the Monroe Doctrine. I LOVE the Monroe Doctrine! I would DIE for the Monroe Doctrine! I just said I didn't know what it was.'

11 September 2001

Greeks certainly know suffering, including several horrendously savage Nazi massacres during World War Two (compensation is today being sought by relatives of victims). More recently, in November 1997, 58 tourists, 18 of them Greek, were gunned down near Luxor, Egypt.

And even more recently, between 20 and 40 Greeks are thought to have died on 11 September 2001 along with an estimated 3,000 other victims.

The appalling attacks on the USA brought out a lot of good in Greece but some bad as well. Archbishop Christodoulos hurriedly clarified what came across as 'God's wrath' comments after uproar in the Greek-American community.

Most ordinary Greeks were deeply shocked at the carnage though not perhaps as deeply sad, seeing it as the inevitable consequence of US foreign policy. A handful of moronic AEK soccer fans burnt the Stars and Stripes and chanted 'Bin Laden, Bin Laden,' which was quite advanced for them.

The government fully supported Washington, as did the main opposition, but opinion polls showed a clear majority of the public opposed to military retaliation against the alleged perpetrators, ageing rock stars Bin and the Talibannies.

Hours after the two planes had smashed into the Twin Towers of New York's World Trade Centre, Communist leader Aleka Papariga, speaking for the people (or the five people in every 100 who regularly vote for her party), called on all workers to resist the 'law of the imperialists'.

Sadly, though also predictably, others had even dafter things to say. The CIA was allegedly behind the attack, ran one view, in order to justify future action by the 'American war machine' against their enemies abroad. Pure pottiness of course. Or as my Dad responded when I relayed this theory to him: 'Never thought of that one.'

Note: In a November 2001 opinion poll published in *Eleftherotypia,* 28% of Greeks said they thought the US intelligence services had instigated the September 11 attacks on the USA (sic). The Israelis put in a disappointing performance with less than 8%. Osama Bin Laden's al-Qaeda organisation got 30%.

Ocalan and Imia

Trust & treason

On 15 February 1999 Turkish commandos captured Kurdish rebel leader Abdullah Ocalan shortly after he left the Greek embassy in Kenya. Three years before, on 31 January 1996, Greece and Turkey had almost gone to war.

Turkish Prime Minister Bulent Ecevit insists that Abdullah Ocalan's human rights will be respected whilst he is tortured in prison though very few international observers believe the PKK chief is currently enjoying a choice of cereals in the morning.

The Ocalan affair cost Theodoros Pangalos, Greece's most talented politician in a generation, his job at the foreign ministry. There were inane charges of betrayal but Pangalos, so controversial that even his (many) apologies tend to offend, would never have created such suspicious circumstances.

No one can yet fully explain Ocalan's 'ambush' on the way to Nairobi Airport. Don't rule out simple blundering, such as the alleged use by Ocalan of a satellite phone which was traced by Turkey, reportedly with US or Israeli help, to the grounds of the Greek embassy in Kenya.

It was the end of a long, dramatic hunt which had started with Ocalan being chucked out of his long-time base in the Bekaa Valley (after Turkey threatened Syria with war), only to seek refuge in Russia (via Greece), Italy and Russia again. Back to Greece, followed by a failed attempt to be allowed into the Netherlands, Ocalan then returned to Athens, went to Corfu (where his military jeep allegedly hit the wing of the plane he was about to take off in) and was finally sent on his way to Kenya by a worried Pangalos. A justifiably bemused Ocalan – fighting for his life, remember – called Turkey the 'terrorist' state and Greece the 'comedy' state.

Other heads also rolled, including those of the interior and public order ministers, and the leader of Greece's secret service, Haralambos Stavrakakis, whose cleverly disguised code name in vital messages to the Nairobi embassy was 'Mrs Katehaki'. Can you guess which street in Athens houses the secret service? And it ain't Mrs Street. How long did Turkey's finest code-busters, armed with super computers and an A-Z of the Greek capital, take to crack that one?

The nation's deep anguish over the capture of Ocalan was best summed up by a friend: 'We had him here in Greece and now Turkey's got him.' Millions of Turks celebrated with genuine joy at having finally captured the 'baby-killer', as Ocalan is routinely called, blaming him for almost 30,000 deaths and ignoring Turkish troops 'eliminating' Kurdish villages. For Greeks, and some others as well, Ocalan remains a remarkably brave man, standing up for a long-repressed people.

Greek Premier Costas Simitis, in bed with reported flu in the closing stages of the crisis, showed considerable political courage. It was not worth entwining Ocalan in the messy morass of Greek-Turkish relations – not worth it for Greece *or* the Kurds. Greece did not have the luxury of distance, the military force or economic might to deal with the inevitable Turkish threats which had already proved too troubling for Russia and Italy to offer Ocalan any permanent home. It was a basic strategic mistake by Ocalan and his supporters to look to Greece for protection. Respect, yes. Protection, sorry.

We can only hope that the government was smart enough to switch Ocalan whilst he was in Athens so that Ankara now has an impostor hanging upside down on Ocalan's exclusive prison-island. I have always been struck by the similarities between government spokesman Dimitris Reppas (when he had his moustache) and Ocalan. If Reppas is the one in chains, his Turkish interrogators are going to be disappointed with responses like: 'I dealt with that point in the previous question. Next!' What's more, as a dentist he might be better able to cope with some of the alternative tactics used by his questioners. Such a switch would explain why the government spokesman, when asked what the cabinet plans to do about improving air quality in Athens, urged a full-scale rocket attack on Turkey.

For the past few years Greece has been easily winning the diplomatic battle against Turkey. A modern, competent, progressive government has put Greece's practical interests first by putting Greece's emotional interests second. It has been a bad week for the country, without any doubt, but it has not been a shameful one.

◪ Apart from Greece and Turkey being within minutes of going to war with each other in the Aegean over Imia [as both countries' naval forces faced off in 1996] it was a very quiet week.

Critics of Greece's climbdown in the Aegean – including those who openly called Prime Minister Costas Simitis [then in office for less than a month] a traitor – say that by giving way on Greek territory today, however deserted, the government is inviting trouble tomorrow.

But all countries make decisions on what to fight over. Even with, as one colleague suggested, a referendum of the goats on the people-challenged islet of Imia (what Turkey claims as Kardak), this was *not* worth potentially tens of thousands of lives in the event of an all-out war. It was bad enough that three Greek navy pilots died when their helicopter crashed. And much more Greek sovereignty could have been lost by fighting a better-armed and bigger enemy than by not fighting at all.

As in marriage or robbing a bank, compromise or even climbdown is sometimes crucial. In a week's time Simitis' decision will be looked on as not so dreadful, in a month as not that bad, in a year as perhaps the right one in the circumstances and, in a decade, as very wise and brave. Which it was.

Note: The first piece, *Sorry I was late, says Ocalan's cabbie*, appeared 21 February 1999. Ocalan was quickly sentenced to death by Turkey. He is still alive, as of the 2001 Christmas Sales, but probably not very happy. The second piece, *Blessed are the peacemakers*, was published 4 February 1996. Over five years on, the wisdom of Simitis' decision not to fight is overwhelmingly, yet silently, accepted by most Greeks. No territory has been lost.

Diplomacy, Poker and Mrs Campbell

Playing chess in front of the world

The Imia crisis, end January 1996, left a bitter taste. Most Greeks thought the EU had chickened out of taking sides and relations with Brussels were consequently strained. A few helpful suggestions were in order.

With all the diplomatic poker currently being played between Greece and the rest of the European Union, I've been thinking a lot about another game, chess, and Mrs Campbell, my former chemistry teacher. Chess taught me everything about diplomacy. Mrs Campbell taught me everything about Mrs Campbell.

Most Friday evenings, at exactly half past seven, five of High Wycombe Royal Grammar School's finest players – bright, studious, talented British teenagers, all bound for distinction at Oxford or Cambridge University – and myself would begin our match against a visiting team in the hallowed silence of the Junior Library, a grand name for a classroom with books in it.

The next three hours were full of devilish combinations and tortuous threats while Mrs Campbell, the teacher-in-charge, calmly smoked away in the corner and marked her pupils' big red chemistry books. But come half past ten, with the games just entering that delicate, fascinating stage which chess players love – and that was it. Mrs Campbell wanted to go home, so 'hurry up and finish'. The school founded in 1562 was officially closing in five minutes.

There was no point citing international laws on chess ('Mrs Campbell, honestly, the rooks can't jump over the pawns') or trying a bit of flattery ('I appreciate your strategy, it's extremely clever, but I can only take his knight if I have something to take it with').

It didn't wash. This blunt and likeable Liverpudlian, giving up precious free time for no pay, was having none of it.

And so, to the great bewilderment of our opponents, at exactly 10.31pm and right after the papal smoke wafting across our boards had delivered the message, six kamikaze attacks would be simultaneously launched, upsetting everything we had spent the last three hours preparing for.

What can politicians and diplomats learn from the Campbell Doctrine?

Rule One: Remember, you don't always know what is going on. This applies to foreign governments trying to understand Greece, and to Greece trying to work out the rest of the world. By the way, if anything, our play improved after Mrs Campbell's 'encouragement' to finish.

Rule Two: Assess the threat, even if it's outrageous. You could argue. You could protest. You could appeal to her better side. You could ask Andy, one of our teammates and her son, to promise to tidy up his bedroom. No good. Mrs Campbell had decided. She was going home and she had the key. Her implied threat to lock us all in was credible because quite simply she *would* lock us all in. Reality could not and cannot ever be ignored.

Rule Three: Respect your judges – or at least pretend to.

Rule Four: Listen carefully to what's being said. Each year, my school's open cross-country race began with hundreds of boys assembled in the Old Gym where Jock, the veteran PE teacher, would proceed to outline the course in his incredibly heavy Scottish accent. The race was invariably won by a runner born north of Kirkcaldy.

Rule Five: Recognise your strengths and weaknesses. A king, bishop and knight can't force a win against just a king; your opponent has to help. Only world champions (or superpowers) can go out on a limb because only they stand a chance of finding their way back.

Rule Six: Put Mrs Campbell in your negotiating team. Cyprus would be solved by a quarter to 11.

The grand old man of British chess, Harry Golombek, was once asked his worst-ever move. He said it was a spectacular queen sacrifice which he thought would lead to a stunning victory and earn him the brilliancy prize, which chess tournaments often award for the most impressive win. So he gave up his queen in great style. Gasps from onlookers. His opponent in shock. And then Golombek noticed the long diagonal of his bishop, upon which the whole attack depended, was blocked by a humble pawn. Too late. He had already given up his most valuable piece.

He would never get it back.

◪ Playing chess in smoke-filled clubs and bars around High Wycombe, Home of the Windsor Chair, was perfect preparation for coming out to Greece.

Alas, Hellas is the last refuge in Europe for smokers. Millions voluntarily forfeit years, sometimes decades, of their lives, making the (exaggerated) dangers of the capital's smog seem irrelevant. Greeks smoked a lung-blowing 32 billion cigarettes in 2000. That's nine per pair of lips every day, including babies.

According to a mid-2000 World Health Organisation (WHO) report, Greece has the seventh longest average life expectancy, 72.5 years, out of 191 countries covered, with Japan first at 74.5. (UN figures for 1999, calculated under a different methodology, put Greek men ninth in the world with 75.3 years and Greek women 13th with 80.5). This is all the more impressive – or sad – because on top of the smoking Greeks are now officially the most 'seriously overweight' people in the EU (but with the lowest level of heart disease, thanks, it's suspected, to olive oil). Not counting stillbirths, the country had the highest EU infant mortality rate in 2000. What's more, Greece is second in Europe for road deaths, overtaken only by Portugal, which can't have any roads. How long clean-living and law-abiding Greeks would endure is an unanswerable question but 130 doesn't seem that unreasonable.

Greeks also drink a lot, but since Australians (73.2) came second in the WHO life expectancy table, I don't think we need to worry too much about this.

Note: A senior road safety official said in September 2001 that good (ie law-abiding) drivers in Greece were now 'a dangerous exception'. Stopping at a red traffic light, for example, can cause an accident. Between 1988 and 1998 the number of road fatalities in Greece shot up by 147%.

November 17

Europe's thickest terrorists

Fascist thugs* have murdered their way around the capital since 1975. One day they'll be caught because, well, they're not very bright. This article was written after the 8 June 2000 assassination of Brigadier Stephen Saunders.

Please don't laugh. There now follows a 'serious' conspiracy theory, widely discussed by the press and public alike, as to why members of November 17, who on Thursday morning murdered British defence attache Stephen Saunders, are never caught. No laughing remember.

Here we go: N17 are really Americans or Britons (the theory has a multiple choice element) who assassinate Britons or Americans in order to make it safer for Americans or Britons to live in Athens by forcing the Greek government, a puppet of Britons or Americans, to crack down on everyone but Americans or Britons.

So now we know: Brigadier Saunders was shot dead in rush-hour traffic so that his successor could feel safer when travelling along the same road to work. How thoughtful!

This theory alone suggests that while, after 25 years of total failure, the counter-terrorism efforts must be seriously stepped up, far more needs to be done in the media and educational fields. That said, virtually all Greeks are sickened by the killing and want the perpetrators caught.

I could give you many equally silly conspiracy theories, none of which I believe in but they would fill this column quite nicely and save me a lot of work. Here's one of my own which took 15 seconds: There was a mix-up over Brigadier Saunders' name and rank so that N17 killed 'Colonel Sanders' in order to get his famous recipe. Silly. Offensive. Very childish. False. And Kentucky Fried Chicken will not be amused. But it's just as good as the one above. Tell your friends.

*The original published version of this article said 'fascist wankers' but with US sales and my mother in mind I have tried to tone down the language in this book. N17 claim to be left-wing but obviously aren't.

'Justification' for the murder came in N17's interminable proclamation, very sensibly not faxed to their normal paper of contact, *Eleftherotypia*.

The convoluted text (it took me three hours to read the Greek) has generated the widespread impression of being written by a failed academic, perhaps jealous of his friends' successful careers. Once seen as a young man with a promising future, at around the age of 18 months, life has been downhill ever since.

It's unfair. He's read just as many books as they have. The kindergarten-level 'critique' of Western imperialism is a bizarre mix of the Encyclopaedia Britannica (actually quoted in the proclamation, presumably without permission) and CNN's *Q&A with Riz Khan*.

Enough criticism. For our middle-aged male writer (the proclamation glaringly omits sexism amongst the Wicked West's many sins) life's truly wonderful. At last, he's had something published! Investing in that set of Encyclopaedia Britannicas was worth it. The journalistic rule, 'The longer the text, the worse the writer,' clearly applies to the author of these 13 pages of undiluted crap, unless it's a parody, in which case it's outstandingly brilliant.

It goes without saying – but in this murky area all things need to be explicitly said – that Greece is *not* a centre of international terrorism, despite wild emotional charges from abroad following this latest assassination, the 23rd since 1975. And, yes, Athens remains the safest capital in Europe for visitors and residents alike, no question.

Let me add my personal hatred for the UK and US arming and supporting obnoxious regimes the world over. However, they're not the only ones and murder is rarely the answer anyway, even accepting that a couple of N17's early victims, including a police torturer during the junta, had a dark and disgusting past, *unlike* Brigadier Saunders whom N17 accused of being responsible for the 1999 Nato bombing of Yugoslavia, the collapse of the 1997 Ethiopian-Eritrean peace talks and Greece's early exit from the 1994 World Cup.

As for punishment, when members of N17 are caught, it has to be life in jail. Without Internet access to the Encyclopaedia Britannica, of course.

◪ On 28 May 1997, N17, one of the very few organisations in Greece to publicly claim responsibility for their actions, assassinated shipowner Costas Peratikos in Piraeus. They knew he didn't have a bodyguard, unlike many in the maritime world, and was an easy target.

On 24 January 1994, N17 shot dead former National Bank of Greece governor Michalis Vranopoulos in Kolonaki, an affluent area of central Athens. The banker did have protection but, astonishingly, his bodyguard was off sick (sic) that fateful day, if press reports are to be believed.

On 14 July 1992, N17, too scared to take on armed government bodyguards, fired a rocket at the passing finance minister's car and managed to miss from all of 10 metres. Instead, the rocket killed a student, Thanos Axarlian, aged 20.

In the future, chances of the group getting really revolutionary, such as blowing up dangerous country roads which kill and maim so many Greeks every day, seem remote. Far too much effort for *urban* guerrillas.

Note: An effective way of crippling November 17, and thousands of innocent Greeks as well, would be to ban any two people travelling on the same motorcycle in Athens from wearing crash helmets. This is the preferred mode of attack for N17: One shoots, the other drives; neither can be identified by security cameras or passers-by. To make it work, any such helmeted pair would need to be immediately stopped by police and *imprisoned* there and then, with their motorbike destroyed on the spot. Under the Church FREEDOM FOR ALL (LOCK THEM UP NOW) Act, a pair of riders wearing helmets would attract instant attention, equivalent to having a huge Turkish flag flying from the back of their bike. Their targets would notice them, as would the general public. End of problem?

The Eurovision Song Contest

Rhymes against humanity

Terrible tunes.
Lousy lyrics.
Saturday 9 May 1998.

England's finest security struggled with Europe's worst music on Friday as 25 nations unashamedly rehearsed for Saturday's 43rd Eurovision Song Contest.

Twenty flag-waving Cypriots in Birmingham's National Indoor Arena cheered 20-year-old Michael Hajiyanni through every musical and lyrical trough *(Genesis, Universal truth, Resurrection of light, Spring's dance of freedom, Genesis)* and graciously clapped the equally dreadful Turkish entry. Three lonely Norwegians unfurled a 'Victory for Norway' banner on hearing Lars Fredriksen howl *Alltid sommer*. This could well be the fifth time Oslo gets no points at all.

Despite, or because of, the dire nature of most songs, organisers claim to be expecting up to 300 million TV viewers worldwide, including Australia, Canada and Korea. All votes, except the jury-led Hungary, will be decided by the public phoning their national broadcaster. You can't vote for your own country, unless you happen to be living abroad...

It promises to be one of the most colourful contests in years. Germany's cult entry, Guildo Horn and the Orthopaedic Stockings, has brought hundreds of supporters to Birmingham – many of England's Euro-sceptics could be forgiven for thinking that *Guildo loves you* is just what the EU deserves on Europe Day. Thalassa, with Patras-born Dionyssia Karoki singing *Secret Illusion*, should enjoy a respectable showing for Greece, particularly with no bouzouki in sight.

Favourites United Kingdom, hopefuls Dutch and the scandalous Guildo wowed those 'lucky' enough to have been let in to watch the trial run. Around 4,000 will be there for the real thing.

Security is always tight for any major UK event, not that terrorists are queuing up to have their name associated with Eurovision '98. The draconian measures are partly a dress rehearsal for next week's G7 summit when presidents Clinton, Kohl and Chirac will be in Birmingham. Thankfully, the only music heard then will be national anthems.

(The day after)

Either Europe has far more transsexuals than anyone could have ever imagined or the controversial Dana International won because voters liked the music and also wanted to annoy the hell out of Israeli Prime Minister Binyamin Netanyahu.

The praise from Israel has certainly been restrained. President Ezer Weizman said it was 'very nice' that 'the state of Israel won first prize'. Not the former Mr Yaron Cohen, now the world's most famous singing transsexual, mind, but 'the state of Israel'.

At a press conference on Sunday, Dana, 26, looking relaxed and radiant despite little sleep after her popular win the night before with the catchy *Diva*, was asked by the *Athens News* if she had received any message of congratulations from Netanyahu. Speaking fluent English, she diplomatically avoided a direct answer: 'Mr Netanyahu spoke last night [on Israeli TV] and he was very happy we won and promised to find the correct budget for [hosting the competition] next year.'

Dana, who had the sex-change operation five years ago, was asked if she had a boyfriend: 'No [...] A few years ago he [her unnamed boyfriend] was the love of my life. [Now] I cannot combine career and love together.'

She won a nail-biting contest in which the world waited to see who would get the 12 points from FYROM, the very last vote of the very last voter. If Malta, that tiny island had won. But it was Croatia and the celebrations in Tel Aviv's Rabin Square began. At the nearest pub to the host venue, a group of Israelis waved flags and ignored baiting from traditionally drunk English locals whose sophisticated repertoire of chants included 'She's a man' and, rather more rudely, 'Cock in a frock'.

Note: In its worst-ever showing, the Greek entry received no points whatsoever except for the customary maximum from Cyprus. Greece also gave Cyprus 12. Put in a difficult position, and no doubt trying to be fair, Turkey awarded Cyprus and Greece the same number of points. Zero. Cyprus ended up with 37 points and Turkey 25. Some other results from Euro '98: Norway 79, the Netherlands 150, Switzerland 0, UK 166, Malta 165 and Guildo 86. In 2001, Greece deservedly pulled off its best-ever finish when Antique came third with *Die for you*.

CHAPTER FOUR

An Interview With the Earl of Elgin (and Other 'Criminals')

Actually he was very nice.
They all were.
Even the one I woke up.

The Earl of Elgin

Sometimes I wish he'd never taken them

This rare interview with the great-great-great-grandson of 'the man who stole the Parthenon' 200 years ago took place in April 1997 at the family's ancestral home in Inverkeithing, Scotland.

Honouring family tradition, the 11th Earl staunchly defended the 7th Earl's actions but the interview ended with some encouraging words for the campaign to bring the 'Elgin Marbles', part of a fifth century BC 160-metre frieze adorning the temple on top of the Acropolis, back to Athens from its 'current' location in the British Museum in London.

Do you ever get fed up that the name of Elgin is always associated with the Marbles? When you say 'Elgin', someone automatically thinks 'Marbles', like Laurel & Hardy.

It's gone on now for so long that we're quite accustomed [to it]. The curious thing is, of course, that as the years have gone by, as the centuries have passed, all sorts of additional aspects appear [...]

Five years ago, my good friends in the British Museum said: 'You'll be interested to know that the plaster models made by your ancestor's agents are now being [...] used to provide information to the Greek authorities, who have found that the remaining sculptures in the Parthenon are now eroded beyond remedial action.'

You feel, with the turn of now two centuries, the whole purpose of the ancestor is vindicated. That's what it was for. That's why he did these things. Let them [the critics] shout, let them rail.

Have you visited the Parthenon?

Once. In 1932 [aged 8].

And more recently to Greece?

Only as a stage through to elsewhere. My passport says I'm Bruce [his family name, related to Robert the Bruce] so they haven't the faintest idea.

You didn't have a hard time with Greek customs?

(Laughs) I was in Istanbul and the museum guide had been told I was someone terribly important but he didn't know who. He said: 'Your Excellency, we have here an even finer collection of Greek statuettes than that of Lord Elgin.' The rest of the party burst into laughter while I was led off.

You weren't tempted to take them back with you?

(No answer)

Does your keen interest in history make you more sympathetic to the Greeks asking for the Marbles to be returned on the grounds that they're a central part of their culture and heritage?

Yes, it's a very good point [...] But though I may have sympathy, it gets tempered by what has actually happened. During the time that there has been much song and dance over the reason why the Marbles of the Parthenon should be returned, you'll find that the remaining statuary on the Parthenon has eroded beyond repair.

Independent experts have no fears now about what would happen to the Marbles if they went back.

It's too late. Why wasn't something done in the previous two centuries? Why weren't plaster models made by Greek authorities?

Imagine Greece saying to you: 'Okay, we haven't looked after the Parthenon very well, like the British haven't looked after Nelson's Column very well. It's now 1997 and the people want the Marbles back.'

Nelson's Column, bless its little heart, has no artistic merit of any sort but what it does have is a great emblem of pride.

I would agree that you get to a moment when it's nothing to do with the artistic, it's nothing to do with the fact that the sculptures which came to the country have been very much better off as part of the British Museum [...] but there is an element of pride. Is it absolutely pure, this pride, or is it politically motivated?

I suppose the question is: 'Are these things not of interest to the whole world?' After all, the world has taken upon itself an enormous number of Greek things like democracy and other words which meant a huge amount, really immensely important things, which were not carvings and stones but were carvings in men's attitudes to themselves. Are all these to be returned to Greece? Are we not supposed to enjoy them? (Smiles)

The Greeks in their generosity would say you can keep all [of] them but the Marbles belong in the Parthenon.

The answer is almost entirely political now. It's been taken out of the realm of the curator [...] It was a moment in history [for the 7th Earl] in which you could have either shrugged your shoulders and turned away – and there would probably be nothing of any consequence left – or you made some great effort.

Maybe it was the last of its kind ever to be envisaged by a private individual. In subsequent history of course governments would probably mount [archaeological restoration] expeditions with very stringent rules to ensure that items remain in the various countries.

It seems clear that very few Britons are interested in the Marbles whereas 99% of Greeks want them back. Where's the problem?

If you say this was our flag, and all the rest of it, why was the flag not properly looked after? [Why not] even sheets hung over it [the Parthenon] to stop the pollution getting at the stone? I couldn't understand it. I still to this day don't and, if I could get a straightforward answer, this other aspect of deep moral pride and feeling might perhaps take a precedent.

There are two sides: The practical side and the side of emotion. The emotional one has always been very well stated [...] One has to admit that even in my lifetime I've had both sides of the emotional one. One says keep them here, another that it's utterly essential that in this new museum [in Athens] one should be able to see the Marbles, provided the custodians are not on strike.

Of course you appreciate the tremendous popular feeling [for the return of the Marbles] but, at the same time, perhaps a little voice from somewhere might say: 'Look, we really are tremendously grateful that we have something to argue about.'

Melina Mercouri [who died in 1994] fought passionately for the return of the Marbles. How did you find her campaign?

(Whispers) Deadly boring. I'm sorry. She stood with the backdrop of the Parthenon in the gap which everybody knew had been blown up by the Venetians and said, 'Look what Lord Elgin did!' I had the pleasure of meeting her husband [film director Jules Dassin]. All these people are charming, very interesting but it's up to the politicians now – on both sides.

Any advice to Greek campaigners?

You've talked about a museum. Alright, build a museum. You'll have lots of gaps in it and people will draw their own conclusions. It may be that it would be better if the gaps were filled than otherwise.

With the Marbles?

Yes. Slowly. It's like water dripping on the stone.

Do you ever find yourself wishing the 7th Earl had just stayed away from Athens?

Yes! (Laughs) Dear oh dear! I think we all do really.

Note: Historian William St Clair revealed in 1998 that the Marbles had been damaged by a disastrous 'cleaning' exercise by the British Museum in the late 1930s, which was then kept secret for 60 years. In Greece, actual construction of a long-delayed Acropolis Museum – intended to house the 2,500-year-old Marbles when, or if, they are returned to Athens – is now planned to start spring 2002. The aim, supported by all political parties and Alain Delon, is to have the $50 million museum fully finished by the time of the Athens Olympics. Given this specific target date, and the huge backlog of embarrassment carried by the project, it possibly will be, providing the 2004 Games are held in Athens (and in 2004 – see Page 95). Greece has now proposed sending Britain other archaeological gems (hopefully including my friend's vase – see Page 16) in return for a 'long-term loan' of the Marbles.

◪ Arriving 30 minutes early for the interview, I asked the taxi driver to drop me off outside of Broomhall, Elgin's mansion.

Major mistake. The 'driveway' lazily winds its way through his impressive 2,000 acre estate (around 900 hectares) and I only just arrived in time, out of breath and exhausted. Cutting across the fields would have been far quicker, but you can't, can you?

Afterwards, the impeccably polite Earl, 73, offered me a lift back to the railway station. To the road would have been more than generous.

Garry Kasparov

Yes?

Imagine the millions of chess players on this planet all lined up in order of ability. Nigel Short, once second in that massive procession, lives in Athens. But in 1998 I got to interview the guy standing in front of him.

World Chess Champion Garry Kasparov will base his new web site in Athens.

Speaking late Wednesday night from his Hilton Hotel suite, Kasparov told the *Athens News* he was in Greece to discuss Club Kasparov, 'a total chess solution' designed to help enthusiasts around the globe improve their game. The operating structure of the 'long-term project' will be based in Athens: 'I have partners here giving technical support.'

The Internet venture is no surprise. Hundreds of chess books, computers and competitions already bear the name of Kasparov, the highest-graded chess player in history. That grade didn't prevent Kasparov from being sensationally beaten in spring 1997 by IBM's supercomputer, 'Deep Blue', now retired, in what was widely proclaimed as a triumph of machine over man. Kasparov has since accused the IBM team of lending a 'human hand' to the machine's calculations and it was clear the defeat still rankled.

The chess ace insisted, 'A machine is a machine, there are many possibilities of manipulation [...] IBM have promised publicly to release printouts [of the machine's processes] for a year now and they haven't.'

This was not the first trip to Greece for Azerbaijani-born Kasparov, who became the youngest-ever world champion in 1985, aged just 22, after defeating his bitter rival, Anatoly Karpov. On Corfu, in 1996, Kasparov played 30 players at once, and won every game except for two draws. A decade earlier, he was part of the victorious Soviet team at the Chess Olympiad held in Thessaloniki.

The legendary Bobby Fischer (see Page 101) is the player to whom the 'Beast of Baku' is most often compared. Fischer visited Athens in 1968, moving hotels four times in one week on account of 'the noise, the noise'. Being based in Moscow, Kasparov said this didn't bother him, adding he would be back later this year.

◪ Apart from the scarcity of actual quotes from Kasparov, indicating a short interview, there was that pliable phrase, 'Speaking late Wednesday night'. What did it mean?

Early Wednesday evening, my Editor excitedly told me he'd come across Kasparov in an Athens hotel lobby. I rang that hotel. Kasparov was out. I then called back every hour until finally, at around 1.30am and Thursday's paper already printed, the receptionist told me Kasparov had just returned. The message asking him to call me had been passed on.

After 10 minutes, I rang again and the magnificent receptionist attempted to put me through: 'He's not answering, sir. I'll try his other phone.' This time, from what was presumably his bedroom, Super K answered. A slightly disoriented 'Yes?' and we were away. A true gentleman – contrary to his general reputation – Kasparov apologised for not ringing back. I didn't have the heart to keep him chatting for long. The poor guy sounded tired.

Note 1: Garry Kasparov's 15-year-long reign as world champion ended in November 2000 after a 15-game battle against Vladimir Kramnik in London. Kramnik is due to play 'Deep Fritz', early 2002, in the latest man-versus-machine showdown.

Note 2: Most Athenians of course do not live in luxury hotels but in large apartment blocks, which are normally very close to the street. The occasional lack of privacy is unsurprising. Indeed, for the 18 March 2001 census, more accurate results would have been obtained not by asking people about themselves but rather what they knew about their neighbours. My once-in-a-decade visit from the Statistical Service came at 8.40 on a Sunday morning. The census-taker first went next door to the general manager of the building who had the sense to warn (and wake) me in advance by two sharp rings of the bell. Suddenly realising that this was literally an in-house survey – and not a casual on-the-doorstep chat – my course of action was clear. That said, I felt a bit embarrassed at getting the vacuum cleaner out, particularly as they could hear it next door. In the kitchen, perhaps uniquely, some unwashed plates may well have dated from the time of the last census.

Michael Dukakis

It wasn't the best of campaigns

Two Greek-Americans have come seriously close to the Oval Office: Nixon's vice president, Spiro Agnew, and Michael Dukakis, the 1988 Democratic presidential candidate. At a September 1996 press conference, Dukakis looked back on his doomed campaign.

Channel 5 were late setting up their mike, the star guest's headphones didn't work and some of the media had arrived at 11.30 when in fact the start had been delayed to midday.

It was almost as if we were again living through Michael Dukakis' famously plagued bid for the US presidency, during which one unkind voter said he was supporting George Bush [father of the current US president, George W. Bush] because he had met Dukakis.

Fortunately, the problems soon sorted themselves out, allowing Dukakis, a three-term Democratic governor of Massachusetts, to meet the press at the Hellenic American Union in Athens. Topics of discussion included the 1988 election, one of the dirtiest (Bush) and weakest (Dukakis) races of the 20th century, and the ongoing stalemate in Cyprus.

Here with his wife Kitty, Dukakis spoke in English after reading an apologetic prologue in Greek. 'My Greek now is very basic,' explained 'Duke'. This was his first visit in 20 years to the land of his father Panos and mother Efterpi, who brought Michael Stanley Dukakis into an ungrateful world on 3 November 1933 in Brookline, a Boston suburb.

The opening question for Dukakis came from a friendly *Athens News*: 'Do you feel pleased or insulted when people say that [US President Bill] Clinton owes everything to you in how *not* to run a presidential campaign?' That campaign included a disastrous tank photo op and Dukakis dying in a debate with Bush after giving a dry 'academic' answer on capital punishment when asked what he would do if his beloved Kitty was raped and murdered.

Pause. 'Well, I would say this: If there's one contribution my campaign made to Clinton's [1992] campaign and to every other campaign [it's that] if our Republican opponent decides to wage an attack campaign, which he [Bush] did against me, we will no longer attempt to shrug it off. [...] If there was one great mistake I made in 1988 it was [in] refusing to respond to that kind of campaign.'

In a reference to the famed 'War Room' in Arkansas, Dukakis, looking good at 62, added that Clinton had set up a 'defence department' in 1992 whose sole function was to strike back immediately when attacked by Bush.

The difference in terminology suggests Dukakis, far more principled than Clinton, was never cut out for the brutality of US presidential politics, even against a tongue-troubled opponent like Bush, who once proudly declared that he stood for 'anti-bigotry, anti-racism and anti-Semitism'.

Loyally defending Clinton's first term in office, especially his handling of the Cyprus issue which has disappointed most Greeks, Dukakis argued: 'I don't know of any president of the United States in my lifetime who's said to the prime minister of Turkey, "This [Cyprus] is personally very important to me" and that's what he said to Ms [Tansu] Ciller [...] I can't remember an administration that's attempted to do more.'

Asked if Greeks should care about who wins the November [1996] election – Clinton faces a Bob Dole so desperate, according to comedians, that he's begun putting his campaign stickers on bananas – Dukakis said that Clinton was 'much more likely to try and move forcefully' on issues important to Greece.

Urging all these efforts along, noted Dukakis, will be millions of Greek-Americans, now more united than ever. 'Bill Clinton has had very strong support from the Greek-American community. He knows that and appreciates it.'

Recalling that in 1988 'there were even a few Greeks who didn't vote for me', Dukakis smiled his sad Snoopy smile and looked like a man who has long since forgiven them.

◪ A Mr William Jefferson Clinton, who gave his occupation as president of the United States of America, came to Athens in November 1999.

His visit triggered mini-riots in the city centre, allegedly in protest at the US-led bombing of Serbia earlier that year, although the two elderly Greek ladies whose toy shop was attacked claimed they had nothing to do with it.

More than anything, the visit demeaned language. All sides were as guilty as sin. Protesters shouted, 'Clinton murderer,' while the president, many blocks away and no doubt remembering, 'It's the Acropolis, stupid!', made non-stop references to 'Home of Democracy' and 'We're all Greeks'. A wordy apology for America's (and Spiro Agnew's) backing of the 1967-74 military dictatorship in Greece went down well.

Although Clinton's visit was reduced from the original four days to an overnight stay, the government later insisted that substantive talks had taken place, and praised interpreters for speaking quickly.

Clinton was to have watched a theatrical adaptation of Tolstoy's *War and Peace*. Instead he saw part of a performance by the Five-Minute Theatre Company and laid the foundation stone for a new bomb-proof Harry Truman statue which is traditionally attacked and defaced because the 33rd US president gave Greece billions of dollars.

Note: The toy shop never reopened.

Gerry Adams

I've never killed anyone

A controversial figure in Northern Irish and British politics, Sinn Fein leader Gerry Adams popped over in November 1996 to argue for a united Ireland and plug his book. He took time out to talk to the Athens News.

Gerry Adams, leader of Sinn Fein ('Ourselves Alone'), the political wing of the IRA, has called for a display of 'courage' from Unionist leaders to get the stalled Northern Ireland peace process back on track.

In Athens to promote the Greek-language version of his autobiography *Before the Dawn*, Adams appealed to the parties representing the Protestant majority in Northern Ireland: 'What we're saying to the Unionists is: "Let's seek agreement, let's talk. Let me put our views, our vision, our fears, our objections on the table." Let the Unionists do the same [...] Let's isolate the issues of disagreement.'

Adams, 48, was asked what it felt like to be the most hated man in Britain in the wake of an IRA attack and his persistent refusal to condemn violence: 'I don't accept that [I am]. I do accept that there's a lot of ignorance, suspicion, fear [...] There has been censorship for a very long time. The only time the people in Britain see or hear of Sinn Fein is, generally speaking, in the context of war or violence or some atrocity [...] Against this I have to say that my personal experience when travelling to Britain has always been to find people welcoming.'

Added Adams: 'Always my conviction is that people in Britain want peace in Ireland.'

Regarding the right of the Protestants in the North to remain in Union with Britain, rather than be forced to unite with the (Catholic) Republic of Ireland in the south, Adams said: 'The people of whatever religious persuasion [...] have the right to be there and no one has any more right to the island [Ireland as a whole] than anyone else.' The reason for the 'siege mentality' of the Protestants 'is because they know the British government will dump them expediently when that moment comes'.

Earlier at a press conference, Adams had been asked whether he agreed that it was now time for both the British government and the Irish Republican Army to make a positive move. 'Eighteen months [of an IRA ceasefire, from end August 1994 to February 1996] is a long time,' responded Adams.

'The IRA ended its campaign on the basis that there would be talks. Imagine this situation anywhere else in the world if such a space was created – for a year and a half – but there were no talks.'

Did Adams, inquired one journalist, expect to see a united Ireland in his lifetime? He did. How long, wondered the *Athens News*, did he expect to live? 'God knows,' came the not-so-religious reply.

The one-on-one interview ended with a triple whammy about Adams' alleged past life as the commander of the Belfast Brigade of the Provisional IRA. Well-rehearsed or genuine, the answers were delivered without hesitation:

Have you ever known about IRA bombs in advance?
No.

Have you ever personally killed anyone?
No.

What's your favourite colour?
Green.*

[Ed: Mr Church's last question was actually, 'Have you ever been a member of the Provisional IRA?' to which Mr Adams replied, 'No'.]

◪ Not counting any bombings/shootings/stabbings/kneecappings/clubbings that he may or may not have been involved in at the start of the 1970s, violence has always been present in Adams' life. He was ambushed and seriously wounded by loyalist terrorists in 1984. One sympathetic profile records that his brother-in-law was killed by British troops, and his brother wounded. Adams' home has also been bombed. He remains easily the top target for heavily armed Protestant extremists.

All that you are now about to read concerning the unbelievable security arrangements for Adams' press conference in Athens should be put in the context of that last paragraph. Ready? Here goes: Three metal detectors, intimate body searches, sniffer dogs, bomb sensors, 20 armed policemen in the building and hundreds outside, roadblocks, an ambulance with its engine always running, quadruplicate proof of ID required at the press office a whole *month* in advance, seats taken up an hour before the start and no tape recorders allowed, non-stop video surveillance and a hugely visible phalanx of intimidating bodyguards.

None of that. In fact...nothing. Not a sausage.

I walked off a main road into the building hosting the press conference without a guard or detector in sight. Up the stairs and still no one. I was only briefly stopped at the door by an event organiser – and that was merely to ask my name and to give me a press pack. And there was Gerry.

Greece, I suspect, has long operated an outrageously successful double bluff on security. You can't see any so you conclude it's very good. Understandably, Greeks are a bit sensitive on this issue, not wanting to be seen as a soft touch, even though it reflects resoundingly to their credit. It's not a violent society, they don't expect attacks and they're not as suspicious about people as the rest of us. In other words, they're normal.

Note: a) The original *Athens News* report on Adams' visit was co-written with Derek Gatopoulos. b) History will quite rightly credit me with solving Northern Ireland. Shortly after I interviewed Adams, a series of compromises on both sides took place and the inane centuries-long conflict is now heading towards a slow but possible conclusion, give or take a few atrocities. Towards the end of 2001, the IRA said they had started 'decommissioning' their weapons. c) Who is Derek Gatopoulos?

Richard Branson

Perhaps I should be more ambitious

Britain's busiest businessman visited Greece in March 1997 to argue his case for building a luxury hotel on Hydra. Charming as ever, Branson faced only one serious problem: Like Ned Kelly, he had forgotten to cover his legs.

The man who would be king – of England at least, if not Hydra – had arrived.

Richard Branson, whom polls show is most Britons' choice for president if the queen is ever dismissed and forced to fly easyJet, was only 25 minutes late. For a press conference partly on airplanes, this seemed appropriate.

Casual suit, no sign of a tie, deranged eyebrows, hair the colour of a miserable autumn in Warsaw, trademark goatee, ever-present smile and at least a billion dollars in his wallet. You couldn't miss him.

There was an almost surreal twist at Athens' spacious Grande Bretagne hotel when one journalist quickly complained about the lack of legroom on a Virgin flight two years ago. Intriguingly, it was the only question of the day which flustered the PR wizard. Branson looked unamused, the Virgin Atlantic manager in Greece said it wasn't really a Virgin jet and would he try the airline again, please? Was that a hint of a free ticket, in which case we all knew what the next 50 questions, including my seven, would be about? No, but the journalist had a follow-up, raising fears he was going to moan about the in-flight movie. Mercifully he didn't.

Legs apart, Virgin has been a disappointment in Greece, with fares nowhere near as attractive as some of their UK-US transatlantic bargains. Indeed, an Athens-London Virgin ticket is often not much cheaper than one from Olympic Airways, the state-spoilt monster which has so many employees they could carry their planes, yet alone fly them. (Consistently cheaper than both OA and VA is easyJet, a regular advertiser with this paper.)

Cornered by the *Athens News* at a post-press conference buffet, the 46-year-old light eater was asked if he ever got bored with business. 'I don't really think of business as business. I see it as a way of life. I enjoy it very much. Tremendous variety.' Branson refused to be drawn politically even though he almost certainly supports Tony Blair's 'new' Labour Party. He does not want to be a politician. Entering the House of Commons 'would be like going back to school and I hated school'. Branson left at 15 – 'I wasn't there long' – and shortly after started building the Virgin empire.

Remarkably, the flamboyant Virgin group of companies has a leader who is at heart deeply shy – quite something for a man who once played himself on *Baywatch*. Cynics say Branson likes meeting the local coastguard, usually after a sudden end to an unsuccessful attempt to go round the world in a balloon.

Branson confessed he doesn't enjoy making speeches. 'I'm not very good at them. I keep on thinking, "Why on earth would anyone want to sit and listen to me?" I rush through as quickly as possible.'

Any ambitions left? 'I haven't got any "I really want to reach this goal in 20-years-time" ambition. There isn't one massive goal we're searching for. Maybe this is a mistake. I was thinking the other night, maybe you should have something.'

Note: Branson, who was knighted in 2000, lost his battle to build a hotel complex on the vehicle-free island of Hydra. Forbes magazine (3 July 2000) estimated Sir Richard's fortune at $3.3 billion though others have put it much lower and one or two have even cast doubt on the overall viability of his global operations which include an appalling train service in England. easyJet continues to thrive and remains as cheerful as ever. One cabin crew member on a flight in July 2001 signed off thus: 'We hope you enjoyed flying with easyJet today. If you did, please tell a friend. If you didn't, let's keep it between us, eh?'

CHAPTER FIVE

A Long Way From High Wycombe: Travels Around Greece

This beautiful country
really has got everything
(apart from public toilets).

Kareas

Putting problems in perspective

So which is the best island for a holiday? Apart from Crete, of course. What parts of Athens should you avoid? Apart from Kareas, of course. And what's wrong with Kareas anyway?

He might have grown up in High Wycombe, Home of the Windsor Chair, but the way my misspelt namesake Bryan casually threw his anchor overboard, without a second's hesitation, was the defining test of a true islander.

That carefree gesture in an enticing cove, at the end of a speedboat journey around the underrated Angistri, showed a man who has long lived life to the full. Incidentally, it also helped explain why the Greek Scuba Diving Association has seen its membership plunge on Bryan's island in recent years.

Angistri, just off Aegina, is around an hour from Piraeus. Typically, Bryan couldn't 'be bothered' to add up the bill at the end of my last stay at his hotel: 'We'll do it next time.' To avoid the newspaper's server crashing due to an avalanche of e-mails from my Scottish readers, here is this book's only plug: Bryan's hotel is called the Agistri Club. (Note no 'n'. Rumour has it Bryan painted the main sign after a few drinks and then kept the spelling this way out of sheer bloody-mindedness.)

Much further away *[Ed: Love the link]*, Lesvos (Mytilene) is another great place to visit, though exercise caution. Molyvos (Methymna) on the left side of this Aegean getaway is superb but you can end up in a tourist trap, a shanty town for the well-off, on the way.

My hotel was actually in the small harbour of Molyvos. Standing on the balcony at 5am in the freshest air around as the fishermen brought in their night's catch was unforgettable.

Out walking in this militarised area, my brother-in-law Paul had the cheek to use an army toilet. Spotted and captured without a fight, the soldiers let him off. In my opinion, they should have shot him.

Also in this region, check out Samos and The Mastic Republic of Chios (see Page 85), home of my personal favourites Maria and Lily. Both are impressively distinctive (I'm referring to the islands) and well worth a couple of nights (see previous parenthesis).

In the Cycladic part of the Aegean, wild Mykonos, the popular gay, straight and sideways resort, is not as out-of-control as generally portrayed. The extinct volcano effect on Santorini is exaggerated – okay, I admit, I've never quite worked out where the explosion happened – but there is undeniable beauty, and the town of Oia is cool.

It's true that none of these destinations are particularly suitable for young children, except for (supervised) swimming and some horse-riding perhaps. Equally impractical for families, late September onwards is the best time to holiday in Greece: Fewer vacationers and a more merciful heat.

If you can, go by boat – the best form of travel – though don't expect too much luxury. Happily singing and scrubbing away, a friend was dismayed to see a floating toilet brush at the bottom of the shower in his 'first-class' cabin.

And the greatest island of all? Two gorgeous women, united by a complete rejection of myself, came from opposite sides of Crete, that slinky sausage sizzling at the bottom of Greece. One worked in Iraklio. After an innocent coffee in Athens I wanted a go on an outdoor lift, the glass bubble type where you can look out on people as you go up. I really enjoyed it but, between us, I think she just thought I was a very childish 31-year-old.

Hania, western Crete, is the loveliest place in Greece for the port alone. Oh the port!

Frankly, there is nothing wrong with the Minoan miracle. Ignore those jealous Athens press reports in 1999 that a nuclear bomb dropped by a US warship off Crete had lain undetonated in the sea for several years. You'd have thought this was exactly the kind of thing the captain would have noted in the ship's log, *0300: Lost nuclear bomb*, but apparently not.

On the mainland, I've been to the northern city of Thessaloniki once – in 1999. Travelling with me was a suitcase stuffed full of prejudice against an occasional bastion of nationalism and Macedonian madness, along with an instinctive dislike of empire-builders from Alexander the Great to Winston Churchill. (What's more, I hold the heretical view that modern-day Greeks are far greater than their ancient predecessors.) Surprise! Salonica was everything Athens isn't – organised, clean and quiet, perhaps a touch dull, with very friendly locals and the sea slap-bang in the appealing centre.

Dropping a few centimetres to the left on a map, through Larissa (where farmers' tractors have blockaded motorways and bishops fought in church – are they bored or *what?*) and Delphi (don't miss the stadium at the top), we land in a big lovable blob called the Peloponnese.

Kalavryta is depressing. Dominated by a war memorial on the edge of town to remember a Nazi massacre of almost 1,500 men and boys over 15 on 13 December 1943 at 2.34pm, the church clock stays at that time permanently. The slaughter started after Resistance fighters had killed 81 German soldiers.

To get to Kalavryta, you take a rack-and-pinion train which winds its way through a beautiful mix of trees and streams wrapped around disturbingly steep inclines. You think of death going up, death whilst you're there – the lack of men is a common observation – and death coming back down, though during my return the train driver was discussing a car sale via his radio.

Staying in the Peloponnese, Patras, Greece's third biggest city, goes gloriously mad during its annual carnival celebrations. Loutraki has lots of famous water and the Corinth Canal must have taken a long time to dig. *[Ed: Terrific analysis.]*

The budding Rio-Antirrio bridge will link the Peloponnese with central Greece in the not-too-distant future. If all goes well and Greece ends up with a world-class bridge, the president will officially open the architectural miracle. If things go badly and funds run out halfway across, Evel Knievel will do the honours.

Note: For the under-30s out there, Evel Knievel is a world-famous motorcycle stuntman who was once stopped from trying to jump the Grand Canyon. Now go back and appreciate the last line again.

◪ Chernobyl once declined to be twinned with Kareas on the grounds it would harm their reputation.

I lived in Kareas, southern Athens, for a record six whole months in 1992. Upper Kareas seemed fine, but the bottom part, where I had been entombed, was dark, dismal and dog-dominated. It boasted two main attractions: *Supermarket No. 4*, or possibly 7, and *Cine Kareas*, after a competition was held amongst natives to find an original name. Long closed, it enjoyed its best season when the Lassie movies were showing.

My favourite Athens district, Pangrati, remains authentically Greek with a cosmopolitan sauce and is close to the city centre. Maroussi combines commuting with community and anything further north, including Kifissia, has that rarest of colours: Green. Wherever you are, except lower Kareas, dedicated gardeners have created some splendid flower beds if you look out for them. At the 'core' of Athens, the Plaka-Monastiraki-Psyrri area is becoming increasingly pleasant, with a surprising ability to switch from gaudy souvenir shops to a genuine Greek hang-out, sometimes in seconds. Petralona has character.

On the outskirts of the capital, and of life generally, avoid gigantic Peristeri, western Athens, and the horrible Salamina (Salamis), the site of a famous ancient naval battle in 480 BC (the losers had to live there). To be fair, friends trying to sell property on the island say Salamina is quite nice once you get past the port.

Strange as it sounds, searching for a house to rent is one of the best ways to discover the real, crazy Athens. One prospective landlord took me down some steep, crumbling steps in Metz, next door to Pangrati. At the bottom of these steps, in order to get to the front door, you had to *jump* over a metre-wide and two-metre-deep ditch or walk across the precarious plank.

Looking back, his classified ad should have made me suspicious: *Fed up with Jehovah's Witnesses?*

Note: a) In June 2001, after eight years in Paleo Faliro, the peaceful coastal resort in southern Athens, I moved to Exarcheia, the traditionally anarchic area just off the centre. Under the terms of the contract, I must pay the rent at the start of every month and throw a Molotov cocktail at two or more policemen by the 10th. b) Forest fires, often started by arsonists (79% of whom are married, middle-class Greek men according to one survey), have burnt far too much of the country, especially in the summer, though 2001 was a 'quiet' year. On 2 August 2001 – the Glorious Second – fire broke out in Kareas. No serious improvements were inflicted.

Kos

Little Ben, Big Ben

In 1991, 20-month-old Ben Needham disappeared during a farmhouse holiday on Kos with his family. Five years on, Ben's grandfather gave the tragic tale a tantalising twist: Ben might discover himself.

Ben's in Greece. Ben's in Germany. Ben's on the beach. Ben's with a group of Gypsies. Ben's gone on a day trip to Euro Disney. Thousands of sightings and still no Ben.

In a case that has drawn worldwide interest, Ben Needham disappeared on 24 July 1991 from a playground on Kos, whilst on holiday with his parents and grandparents from Sheffield, northern England. He could be dead, or perhaps abducted, then sold to a childless couple and now almost seven [in 1996].

There is no proof either way despite several widespread searches of the Dodecanese island. Greece is such a non-violent country, the former toddler might indeed be alive and well. But where?

With Ben's mother, Kerry Needham, having had a nervous breakdown and his father, Simon Ward, encountering (legal) problems of his own, all Greeks will admire the spirit of his grandparents, Eddie and Christine Needham, who are now leading the campaign to keep their missing grandchild in the public spotlight.

At a press conference held at the British embassy in Athens, Eddie announced that the reward for information leading to Ben's safe return has now been increased to a massive 191 million drachmas [then 530,000 pounds sterling].

Did Eddie think the reward was 'the best chance you've ever had' of finding Ben? 'I honestly do, yeah, because even if Ben is no longer in Greece, the answer to the problem must be still in Greece. The reward is aimed at someone who may have been involved or knew someone involved in the disappearance of Ben.'

And if nothing comes up? 'We'll never stop searching for him, never give up searching for him because he has to know the truth of what happened.'

Asked by the *Athens News* if it would help to know that Ben was actually dead, Christine, crying or near to tears for most of the press conference, said it would 'in a way [because] we would know then what had happened'.

For Eddie, 'when someone dies you can lay them to rest [...] and know they are not suffering any more and you know where they are [...] It's just not knowing, five years [now over 10] of not knowing. That is a terrible thing.'

The family has made it clear they would not press criminal charges if Ben turned up alive. 'Just leave him at an embassy or a hospital or anywhere,' Eddie told a similar press conference in 1994. Even by then, endless sightings of Ben-like boys had constantly and cruelly raised their hopes. [By 2001, a reported 200 'serious' sightings had been seriously investigated.]

There was an unexpected twist at the press conference: The one person who might discover Ben is Ben himself, as he grows older, along with indelible birthmarks on the back of his neck and a coffee mark on his right leg. 'With your help,' Eddie told the 50-strong media crew, 'maybe Ben will recognise himself.' He has no doubts that 'we would know him instantly'. And a DNA test would settle everything.

If Ben was watching them now on TV, what would they say? Stumbling for words, and obviously moved at the thought, Eddie held his distraught wife's hand and replied: 'What can I say? He can't understand me anyway. We love you [Ben] very much, we want you to come back to us, that's all I can say. Please get in touch.'

Note: Ben, now entering the difficult teenage years, still hadn't been found by the end of 2001. Possible sightings and all other related information should be given, anonymously if necessary, to the British embassy in Athens or to any Greek/British police station.

◪ If any reader owns an elephant – or has a really good elephant mask – let me know.

Time to explain. Spending the [98-99] New Year with my brother's family in northern Spain, I told niece Lorea, 6, that I live in Athens with three elephants. This was part of our nightly agreement. I tell her a bedtime story if she agrees to turn the telly down so I can get some sleep. Greece included, these Mediterranean kids don't realise just how good a deal they've got.

The elephants are named after her aunts and my sisters, Pat, Sue and Debbie. Lorea giggles. Problem. It's hard watching TV together, I said, because they keep switching channels with their trunks. Super bright, and effortlessly trilingual, Lorea decides to check with my brother, Mike: 'Es true daddy?'

'Fresh' from washing up and taking the rubbish out, Mike is now busy picking up the toys thrown all over the floor (for which I later apologise). But it's an honour for this dedicated English teacher to be consulted and he knows it. Until recently, Mike said the order of power in their Basque household was: Begona (his wife), Joseba (his five-year-old son), Lorea (his daughter), the fridge, himself. This had now changed to: Begona, Lorea, Joseba, the fridge, Mike.

Anyway, my brother says he doesn't know, so Lorea has another idea. She wants me to send her a photo of my trio of elephants: 'And no go to the zoo.'

In the past I've asked for – and received – a 39mm bath plug from readers but this could be the hardest test so far. Yet try I must. Elephants never forget and nor, my brother tells me, does Lorea.

Note 1: I was offered a cuddly 'Jumbo' but no actual elephant mask. Lorea, now 9, has forgiven me but not forgotten. Despite a strong challenge from my brother, the fridge has kept its position.

Note 2: Back a few Decembers, I asked Mike what he was doing for Christmas. His instant response: 'We're doing chicken.' I miss him.

Corfu

If you've time for only one island, this is it!

Sparkling harbours. Intoxicating orange groves. The Jewel of the Ionian is history's loveliest present to the future. No serious traveller can ignore 'Kerkyra' and nor should you.

I have never been to Corfu.

[Ed: I'm not very happy with this.]

Chios

Mastic, Homer and Muhammad Ali

Some people look at things and say, 'Why?' I look at things and say, 'Why not mastic?' (US President John F Kennedy, as reported in Chios newspapers.)

And so to Chios.

I went in spring 1993 to see John Perikos, an authority on gum mastic, that sticky substance which uniquely comes from 'the tree that cries', *Pistacia Lentiscus var. Chia*. What to the outsider looks like a tree trunk dribbling was liquid gold to John with a thousand uses – edible (the world's first chewing gum), drinkable (ouzo), dental (helping prevent gum disease) and even medical.

Many mocked the last claim but the Mastic Millennium could prove John, coincidentally export sales manager of the Chios Gum Mastic Growers Association, to be totally right. Scientists at Nottingham University, England, announced in the *New England Journal of Medicine* (24 December 1998) that 'masticha' was apparently effective in curing peptic ulcers by being active against *Helicobacter pylori*. The team called for more investigation.

Clearly there is something special at work. And John, now a good friend, knew this at the start of the 1990s when he wrote *The Chios Gum Mastic*, with an introduction by Sir Derek Barton, the 1969 Chemistry Nobel Prize winner no less. John has also penned a book on Homer (which, like the gum mastic self-help manual, I helped edit), trying to show the great bard was from Chios. This is quite widely believed on the island and not such an unreasonable assertion. There's even Homer's Seat where Homer used to...sit. Furthermore, John has translated research claiming Christopher Columbus was from Chios – again not impossible – but I've told him I think he's pushing it with Muhammad Ali. ('Chiotes' have a fine sense of humour, and often a lot of money, so it's very hard to offend them.)

Described as 'rugged' by Homer, Chios (HE-os) is interesting for its location as well, being right by Turkey. If Greece had decided to fight in 1996 over Imia (see Page 47), this rocky island might have hosted one hell of a battle with mastic bombs used indiscriminately in blatant violation of several international recipes.

Well known for its crop of nautical giants and various other famous people, like composer Mikis Theodorakis (also claimed by Crete) and statesman George Papandreou, father of Andreas Papandreou, Chios looks big and feels small. The 50,000 inhabitants, blessed with exactly the right proportions of talent, hard work and eccentricity, make the place, which remains largely unaffected by tourism.

During my stay on Chios, we visited two local landmarks: The Chios Gum Mastic Growers Association Headquarters and Nea Moni. This Byzantine monastery openly displays skulls and other bones of victims of the 1822 massacre by the Turks. As many as 25,000 died.

Up to the official-on-duty went John to ask if he knew anything about Iakovos Columbus who was a former priest at the monastery. *When?* In 1519. It was one of the harder questions of his day.

High Wycombe

Home of the Windsor Chair

Fly from Athens to Luton Airport, travel down to London, day-trip sideways into Windsor and drive up again to Oxford. In the middle of that rough square stands High Wycombe, the Mecca of English furniture.

We rate ourselves in Wycombe, it's true. The first sign motorists see after coming off the M40 from London is *Welcome to High Wycombe – Twinned with the United States of America.**

High Wycombe (HW) is of course Home of the Windsor Chair, a landmark in furniture design. My town has even got a picture of the spindle-backed wooden seat on an unlimited edition of mugs. It's probably unique to be famous for something named after somewhere else. You're not likely to see *New York – Home of the Chicago Bulls*, are you? We don't mind. Besides, Windsor's not so far away.

The same modest spirit is seen at our tourist office, which has a large number of leaflets suggesting places to visit in HW, including the Republic of Ireland, Shakespeare's Globe Theatre in London (only half-an-hour by train), walking tours of Oxford and the Silverstone Grand Prix. Until 1946 we were officially called Chepping Wycombe, which was possibly a disgruntled visitor's insult though local historians insist 'Chepping' meant 'Market'. Wycombe, pronounced WI-kum (the WI- as in Wycombe), gets its name from the River Wye and the olde English word *-combe* ('in the mouth of').

Many famous people have lived in the wider area: Political philosopher Edmund Burke (in Beaconsfield), pop star Howard Jones (Green Street, HW – see below), poets Milton (Chalfont St Giles), Shelley (Marlow) and Thomas Gray (Stoke Poges), and children's writers Roald Dahl (Great Missenden) and Enid Blyton (Beaconsfield). TS Eliot once taught at the local grammar school. Kings, queens and Nora Turner have popped by over the years. The age-old Wycombe welcome is to build a huge arch of chairs. Not one has collapsed yet, knock on wood.

*Thank you to the reader who wrote to inform me this wasn't true.

We have a well-known tradition, possibly from medieval times, which is to weigh the new and old mayors in public. The idea is to see if he or she has put on weight since being in office and all that implies. Centuries ago, the guy apparently got plastered with eggs if found to be heavier. According to a semi-official *Brief History of High Wycombe*, spectators nowadays come 'from all over the world' to watch.

Drowning in the green of the beautiful Chilterns, Buckinghamshire's biggest town (population: 60,000) used to call itself 'the furniture capital of England'. Well they wood say that, woodn't they? No, it's true, thanks to generations of skilled craftsmen ('bodgers'), including Steve Redgrave's grandfather (see below). Unfortunately, the industry is in clear decline and the youth of today are no longer interested in that kind of beech.

Some outsiders have dared to call the town 'boring'. They've obviously not been to the Wycombe Chair and Local History Museum in Priory Avenue which boasts 'a world-famous collection of chairs' and 'a 1920s kitchen reconstruction'. Entrance is free but phone ahead in case all seats have been taken.

If the museum is closed, the wise visitor will enjoy the glorious countryside around the village of West Wycombe and its lovely old church, invariably shut, with a big golden ball on top. The Hell Fire Club, aka The Medmenham Monks, used to meet in the caves below and engage in general – as well as pretty specific – debauchery.

More controlled, yet still very exciting, the annual Wycombe Show has often ended in complaints from organisers and exhibitors alike about the poor public attendance, despite the impressive arts and crafts (eg woodwork) on display.

Apathy can be rampant. One march in the 1980s protesting against the longstanding American air force base allegedly ended halfway up one of many steep hills when it began raining.

What else is there? For starters, Wycombe Swan Theatre holds its own nationally. Then there's a dry ski slope, Bekonscot Model Village and Chequers (the British prime minister's country residence), every one within 10 miles (15km).

In Wycombe itself, we also have Castle Hill House, maybe as old as the 17th century. Okay, it houses the Chair Museum. It was worth a try. The film *Four Weddings and a Funeral* was shot in nearby

Amersham – found in the top left corner of a London Underground map – but the original screenplay *Four Weddings and 15,000 Arrests* was set in Wycombe.

Let the word go forth: Wycombe believes in law enforcement. Nowhere else can police get a search warrant because the suspect hasn't taken his milk bottles out. At the Magistrates Court, I personally witnessed a driver being charged with possession of a defective windscreen wiper washer.

Put simply, we're a conservative bunch and not ashamed of the fact. Most Wycombites are against the decriminalisation of cannabis. A third of us think aspirin should be made illegal. Don't get the wrong idea. Civil liberties are not forgotten in this former Quaker stronghold and land of the rebellious John Hampden. Our motto has never changed: 'Innocent Till Proven Guilty. Or Best of Three.'

We respect the military too with major UK-US establishments in the vicinity, starting with RAF Strike Command, say no more. The Royal Military College, better known today as Sandhurst, began life in 1799 in Wycombe High Street, which is still noticeably wide but has more modern institutions. As one council guide notes: 'The building now occupied by McDonalds is a late 18th century Georgian town house.' The prestigious Wycombe Abbey School for girls became the US 8th Army Air Force HQ during World War Two. Just outside Wycombe, Bomber Command, headed by Arthur 'Bomber' Harris, coordinated the destruction of Dresden on the night of St Valentine's, 14th February 1945, killing an estimated 100,000 civilians, possibly higher.

It remains a mystery why HW, despite this massive military presence, was never seriously bombed by the Nazis, being so close to London what's more, and also to Chequers. Unconfirmed gossip at the time claimed Hitler's girlfriend lived down Bassetsbury Lane, next to the cricket ground, and so the Luftwaffe were ordered to leave HW alone. The alternative explanation – every night a massive neon sign at the cricket ground beamed up to passing planes the message LONDON 25 MILES – is not popular locally.

Wycombe Wanderers Football Club enjoyed a sensational cup run in the 2000-01 season, getting as far as the last four in the entire country before narrowly losing to lucky Liverpool. What a difference one year makes. The team, sponsored by a furniture manufacturer, had previously made the news in November 1999 during a cup match against lowly Oxford United. Just as penalties were about to decide the game, a presumed 'Chairboys' supporter had the sense to set the stadium on fire and the game was abandoned. Our brave players, some of whom used to be part of a witness protection programme, won the next encounter.

In the past, Wycombe's managers have asked for their names not to be published. Pre-cup glory, coach Laurie Sanchez blasted the low turnout at home matches and sarcastically claimed more Wycombites would come along if Adams Park, the club's stadium, was converted into a supermarket. His comments caused uproar. Furious ratepayers insisted they would prefer a garden centre or, failing that, a fifth prison. The frustrated manager said they were missing the point. In honour of the 'Heroes of 2001', I have proposed renaming Desborough Avenue, a main thoroughfare in the heart of town, Desborough Sanchez.

Away from sport, Wycombe's games are sometimes broadcast live on HW's only radio station which is called 1170 presumably because more people can remember this number than the town's actual name. A lively press occasionally has job adverts for 'Machine Gunner/Mortar Man/Anti-Tank Gunner' but generally focuses on day-to-day issues (*Panther-like cat on the prowl in garden*) and human interest stories, such as damage to luggage at an airport (*It's plane shocking*). One story about a museum extension was titled *Royal Opening*. And which member of the royal family turned up? 'Nora Turner, dressed as Queen Victoria.'

◪ If Steve Redgrave, who won a fabulous FIFTH consecutive gold medal at the Sydney Olympics in September 2000, is not the greatest Olympian ever, then he is at least the finest oarsman to have come out of High Wycombe.

Striking gold at every Olympics since 1984 is an unprecedented achievement, if we don't count that twit called Aladdin who fluked his way to victory decades ago by waving a silly wand around. *[Ed: Mr Church is referring to Hungarian fencer Aladar Gerevich.]*

Wycombe had pop star Howard Jones living in the town centre well before international fame beckoned. He was one of us. Down-to-earth, approachable, good-natured, even worked in a factory. A truer Wycombe man you couldn't find and affectionate headlines in local papers rejoiced at his success: *Howard's first single on sale today – Howie-about-that! 'New Song' in Top Twenty – Super Sofa Sale Starts Saturday – Howard's star soars – Arrogant Jones abandons High Wycombe.*

To be super truthful, Redgrave is actually from Marlow, an insignificant wasteland along the road. So what? Instead of the Thames, Redgrave might have secretly practised on our very own river, the Wye, although the mini-waterfall at the end requires a degree of caution. And his family regularly shop in Wycombe which is more than enough. He's ours. We saw him first.

CHAPTER SIX

What's the Hurry?
(Good Things Come to Those Who Wait)

The rest can get on the A2 bus to Voula.

The 2004 Athens Olympics

You ain't seen nothing yet!

'The organisers of the Games must present to the watching world a dynamic and technologically advanced capital whilst keeping on-track collisions between athletes and unlicensed peanut trolley vendors to a minimum.'
(Official government contract)

Athens was awarded the 2004 Summer Olympic Games on 5 September 1997. Athens had the 2004 Summer Olympic Games taken away on ___ (readers can fill in this bit for themselves). Just joking. The capital has got the talent to organise a successful Games, no question. And if it wants to screw them up, an awesome arsenal of 'specialists' is also available.

Senior IOC member Dick Pound was asked in October 2000 about delays in construction of the Olympic Village (the cabinet has denied secretly ordering 100,000 hammocks) and about how badly Athens was doing generally. He was foolish enough to say the situation merited '8 to 9 on a [crisis] scale of 10', thus making the entire nation automatically think, 'Well it's not *that* serious, then.' If he's seen paying a secret visit to Athens, watch out for the headline, *Spotted Pound.*

Even the lighting of the Flame at Ancient Olympia ahead of the September 2000 Sydney Olympics degenerated into farce due to minor dignitaries turning up late – thus ruining the chance for the sun's rays to do their job – and some memorable music from a local outfit. Afterwards, Theodoros Pangalos, the no-nonsense culture minister [at the time], publicly asked: 'Where did they get that band?' Some of the Australians present reportedly failed to recognise their own national anthem. Speculation swirled that Athens would get the 2008 Games, if they're still being held, to allow organisers more time to build the Village and replace the brass section.

Unfortunately for the Athens Organising Committee (ATHOC), the 2004 Games became a domestic political issue in Greece on the very first lap. Opposition parties have enjoyed attacking the government on any Olympic-related matter, ie everything, since it's only that magic number of 2004 which 'guarantees' on-time completion of much-needed, large-scale infrastructural works which will last well beyond the Games. The country's environmentalists vehemently oppose the planned rowing event at Schinias. Archaeologists insist the 490 BC Battle of Marathon took place at exactly the same site (without the water). It's now a major legal fight.

A few Greeks don't want the 'tainted' Olympics back. In July 2000, ATHOC were ridiculed for wanting to move from their headquarters after only four months. Forced to share the building with a supermarket, ATHOC understandably argued that briefing the international media with someone shouting 'Kilo of bananas please, darling' in the background detracted from the seriousness of their mission.

If the International Olympic Committee do ever begin talking seriously – say twenty four-and-a-half out of ten – about removing the Games, don't rule out a full-time Olympics government in Greece, one faction demanding more funding for synchronised swimming and the other wanting to bring back one-hand weightlifting as an Olympic sport.

Despite the problems, much is on Athens' side. End 2000 the IOC said talk of moving the Olympics from their birthplace, both ancient (776 BC) and modern (AD 1896), was ridiculous. Moreover, by some estimates, 70% of the major construction projects had been finished by 2001 – 85% if you count the bar for Scottish journalists. Greeks love sport (Greece and Turkey are jointly bidding to host the 2008 European soccer championship) and take great pride in Greece's medal tallies from recent Olympics (four times as many golds as Britain in 1996 with a sixth of the population and one fifty thousandth of taxpayers.) From 13-29 August 2004 (17-28 September for the Special Olympics), the world will see why this country has so many fans. Around 11 million people visited in 2000. My guess is a quarter come every year. Exploring the roots of that exceptional loyalty should condition the focus of the Games. Make them simple. And fun. Relax (radio stations here can announce the year and the time). In other words, make them Greek.

Unfortunately, these attributes are the exact opposite of what you want in *preparing* for the Games. If things go wrong, the damage could be up there with a war, as Atlanta found out in 1996. ATHOC chief Gianna Angelopoulos-Daskalaki, who essentially won the spectacle for Greece after the 1996 bid fiasco, predicts the media in particular will love the 28th Games. Likewise, minister Pangalos, overflowing with that classic American self-belief in success, has said that failure of the 2004 Olympics would be the IOC's responsibility just as much as the Greek capital's.

What about 'security worries'? Super safe for ordinary visitors, Greece has never been in contention for a medal at catching terrorists like the November 17 clowns (see Page 51). Four policemen stuffed into one car outside a major ministry were watching Spain play Italy in the 1994 World Cup quarter final on a small TV. Other guards were likely inside, and the minister not at work, but impressions can count. Xerox, a major US sponsor, has denied wanting the Olympics moved elsewhere, or asking for a copy, maybe three, in different sizes.

On a lighter note, the possibility of poorly guarded entrances to sporting venues is raising concerns that the traditional coin-throwing by Greek basketball fans could trigger an instant court invasion by Scottish supporters at the other end.

Why are the Games unique for Greece? Because they can't be denied, disowned or disputed. They're here. We're responsible. Come August 2004, tourists and athletes arriving at Athens Airport simply cannot be told 'What Olympics?' before the guard walks off to have a smoke with his mates. In the past, Syntagma Post Office could happily release their five-volume, 18,000-page blockbuster, *Summer Closing Hours*. But now we must all be open. For good.

It's a challenge.

Note: Culture Minister Theodoros Pangalos was sacked on 19 November 2000 for derogatory comments about cabinet colleagues (though not on Olympic matters). Supreme waffler Evangelos Venizelos returned to his old portfolio which 'enjoys' ministerial responsibility for the Games. Jacques Rogge, who had been the IOC Coordination Commission chairman responsible for the Athens Games, succeeded Juan Antonio Samaranch as IOC president in July 2001. Denis Oswald took over Rogge's former post and is not considered so Athens-friendly. In September 2001, the IOC strongly criticised venue construction delays and voiced annoyance that preparations only seemed to reach full speed ahead of an official visit to Athens by their inspectors, sarcastically adding they couldn't come every week. A month later, an unconnected cabinet reshuffle saw Premier Costas Simitis assign several deputy ministers to the task of the Olympics. Simitis, rather sadly, says the Games are his government's highest priority. It is not inconceivable that Athens could still lose the Olympics (or, it's been speculated, control of the organisation). Another November 17 strike, statistically due soon, could be fatal in more ways than one. But more likely, the Athens Games will be an enjoyable success.

◪ The official logo for the 2004 Athens Olympics is very nice indeed. A vibrant and daring design enhances an elementary yet attractive idea.

But what is it?

I'm jealous of course. My entry showed a souvlaki-guzzling taxi driver drooling 100-dollar bills as two fat American tourists come wobbling along towards him. The committee of judges said it was 'appallingly racist' though they agreed the cabbie was a touch lifelike.

I don't have much luck with competitions. At university in the late 1980s, Amnesty International asked students to come up with a poster to remind the public of the hostages locked up in Lebanese dungeons. The 'missing' included Terry Waite, the archbishop of Canterbury's special envoy, who had originally tried to free the other prisoners but ended up a hostage himself for almost five years.

Some friends also felt quite strongly about the issue and together we conceived a poster in simple black and white to emphasise the powerful starkness of the hostages' day-to-day *non*-existence. The actual drawing was equally basic: A man trapped behind bars. Nothing else. A few last-minute adjustments – the words *How long must Terry Waite?* at the bottom, a pint of beer held high in the prisoner's right hand and the speech bubble *All the best from Beirut!* – and we were done.

I can't remember if we actually entered it in the end but I can remember that it didn't win.

Rejection

Women hurt but articles wound

The 'Top 10 American Lunatics As Seen By Europe' took some 200 hours to write in June 1999 but, like Maria from Chios, no magazine was interested. Read it once for me. Please?

Forget Charlie Manson. The US should worry about the people it *hasn't* locked up, starting with these 10:

10. Charlton Heston
Controversial president of the powerful National Rifle Association (mission statement: 'Shoot the bastards') and Moses' unofficial representative on earth. With Europe alternately amused and aghast at America's affection for guns, Heston knows he's in the right country. A decade back, one US reporter taken on a drugs bust by London police was horrified to discover on the way that not a single officer had a gun.

9. Madeleine Albright
Anti-communist in a non-communist world, across the Atlantic the US secretary of state can seem a little too keen to don a flak jacket and bring on the big boys. Prague-born Albright once worked for Zbigniew Brzezinski at the National Security Council where she demonstrated her brilliance by spelling his name correctly.

8. Senator Jesse Helms
Seriously deranged in European eyes with an abnormally high interest in communists, homosexuals, liberals and Richard Holbrooke. First elected in 1972, the 78-year-old North Carolina senator chairs the powerful Foreign Relations Committee. Noticeably unpopular on the Internet where sites include *Jesse Helms Must Die* and *Jesse Helms – the Great Satan.*

7. James Carville
The famed Clinton attack dog fulfills one essential pre-condition of any self-respecting lunatic: He thinks others are mad. In 1996 Carville said presidential candidate Ross Perot was 'loony as a

tune. I don't think he's got both oars in the water'. Many Europeans have a problem with the colourful Louisiana vernacular of 'Ragin' Cajun', who is rarely cited in arguments supporting human cloning.

6. Vice Admiral James Stockdale

Locked up (by the enemy) in north Vietnam and tortured for almost eight years, Stockdale gained international fame with an inspired performance in the 1992 vice presidential debate. His now legendary opening line, 'Who am I? Why am I here?', drew audible laughter. Later, the Reform Party candidate went back to the 'Hanoi Hilton': 'We had an acronym, BACKUS, and each one of those B-a-c-k was something for which you – you had to make them hurt you before you did it [...] But at the end it was US, BACKUS. You got the double meaning there.' Whilst millions of watching Americans wondered, wrongly, if the 'C' stood for Cannabis, a wise few glimpsed that rarest of Washington animals: A man with 26 combat decorations and the Congressional Medal of Honor able to keep politics in perspective.

5. Monica Lewinsky

Any student voted 'Most likely to give one to the President of the United States of America' is always going to draw large crowds in Europe, where Lewinsky has seriously considered living according to deeply unserious press reports. Like everyone in the world, Lewinsky was driven mad by Ken Starr's five-year 40-million-dollar inquiry, which proved beyond any reasonable doubt that lawyers have no trouble at all spending 40 million dollars in five years.

4. Rev Pat Robertson

Only Robertson could think of (legally) using two 'Operation Blessing' charity airplanes for a diamond mine venture in Zaire. A blistering attack on Scotland – 'a dark land overrun by homosexuals' – led to pro-life Robertson being aborted in 1999 only weeks into a telephone banking deal with the Bank of Scotland. Founder of the immensely successful Christian Broadcasting Network, Robertson ran for the 1988 Republican nomination, arguing that if Michael Dukakis was the Democratic candidate, everyone should be allowed a go.

3. Waylon Jennings

Forced to accept strange American names (Zebulon Pike, Henry Ford II), Europe has always drawn the line at *Waylon*, no disrespect to the man who brought us the timeless classic *Look Into My Teardrops*. Jennings escaped a fatal air crash on 3 February 1959 – in which Buddy Holly died – after giving up his place to Jiles Perry Richardson, 'The Big Bopper'. An ungrateful Waylon went on to write the theme tune for *The Dukes of Hazzard*.

2. Bobby Fischer

The obnoxious genius has long baffled chess-loving Europeans. US champion at just 14, and blessed with a breathtakingly beautiful style, Fischer was once told by a teacher, upset at seeing his pocket chess set in class, to 'play without the board'. The man who won the intellectual Cold War for America by claiming the world crown against Boris Spassky in 1972 is said to remember every move of every game he has ever played, a feat equivalent to Bosnian Serb leader Radovan Karadzic reciting all his war crimes charges. Certainly Fischer, born in Chicago in 1943, never forgets who his enemies are – those naughty Jews and Mossad's chess division. True to form, early '99 he was thrown off Hungarian radio for 'anti-Semitic remarks'.

1. Ted Turner

Genius and lunacy are first cousins and no one has proved this more than media mogul Ted Turner. Before starting CNN in 1980, pundits predicted that round-the-clock news would be astronomically expensive. Accountants came up with a ballpark figure for Jane Fonda's estranged husband by multiplying the cost of one hour's original material by 24. It was at this point that Turner realised that repeating one hour's worth of original material 24 times would be far more profitable. The silliest ideas are often the best.

Greek TV

Turning the nation on

You might have to wait for your programme since almost nothing starts at the advertised time. But as this TV review from August 2000 pointed out, the wait is often worth it.

Would it have been of any consolation to the late Mr and Mrs Menendez, comprehensively murdered by their loving sons Erik and Lyle in 1989, that a US mini-series about their happy family life together was shown on TV last weekend (Mega, Sunday, 9.05pm)?

Probably not. But they might well have appreciated the white triangle inside a yellow circle appearing on screen before *A Killing in Beverly Hills* began, accompanied by the unintentionally ironic words: *Parental consent required*. So they did not die in vain.

The new list of symbols, seen as a commendable attempt to help parents prevent their kids from watching unsuitable material, or as an even more praiseworthy move to inform consenting adults in advance what kind of smut they can look forward to that night, is just one good reason to watch Greek TV. There are so many more:

Pro-choice

A private zap at 4am Tuesday came up with a Greek film, a US sitcom, MTV, a Chaplin comedy, a football match, close-ups of a couple definitely not discussing the size of their telephone bill, a European arts programme, an old American movie, a repeat of news, Greek music, a promotional video for an exercise machine ('That was me then, and this is me now!') and *Larry King Live* on CNN [shown free in Greece, when the picture is not obliterated by TV Makedonia; Arabic super-station al-Jazeera are rumoured to have the same problem]. On top of every Latin American soap ever made, there's no end (or copyright fee in some cases) to the range, though not depth, of Greek TV. The deaf talk show host always shouting out *Pos?* (What?) to viewers brave enough to call him up is an accidental classic.

Very funny

Nationalism is good for the giggles. On a big Sunday night show, on Mega, one 'comedian' was asked what he'd do if he saw Turkish aeroplanes violating Greek airspace. His witty retort, 'Blow them up', got huge applause. The extreme right-wing stations are even funnier: One viewers' poll showed 97% in favour of sending in the riot police to evict some anarchists from the legal sanctuary of the Polytechnic.

Men in black

Everyone's been talking about the possible separation of Church and State. But what Archbishop Christodoulos really fears is the separation of Church and Television. Neither would ever be the same again. The charismatic leader of the Orthodox Church of Greece once again attracted the most interest this week, despite strong competition from *Gorillas in the Mist* (Star, Monday, 10pm). Ironically, in this advanced, multicolour age of digital communications, both man and monkey looked good in simple black and white.

Morning all

Queen of the Coffee Cup, Antenna's Eleni Menengaki (*Morning Coffee*, Antenna, weekdays, 10am) is even more gorgeous in real life than on screen. You're just going to have to take this writer's word for it. How many TV presenters have an MBA from Harvard and write environmental policy speeches for Prime Minister Costas Simitis? Not many, and certainly not our Eleni, but she's still the greatest.

The power of TV

Apart from millions of violent pornos, stations wisely choose only programmes which re-enforce family values, such as *Walker Texas Ranger* (Antenna, Saturday and Sunday, midday), listed in Greek as *Kick His Head In Chuck* (alright, *Chuck Norris, In the Service of the Law*). If your time is precious, Chuck normally kicks them quite hard at 5, 20, 51, 52, 53 and 54 past the hour.

Oh my Godfrey

Every film under the sun has been shown, is being shown and will be shown on the small screen. If you've enjoyed a movie, and are sad it's finished, albeit abruptly with the credits barely shown, hurry up; it's starting again on another channel. *Their Man* or *Our Man* or *My Man Godfrey*, whatever it's called, has been shown a minimum 500 times in the last 10 years, ie once a week. Most viewers can now follow the plot.

Here is (not) the news...

Despite being the only programme to start ahead of time (and broadcast free of 20-minute-plus adverts), the news served up by major private TV stations is almost invariably sensationalist, nationalist and commendably low-brow (unlike more staid coverage on the three state channels, ET1, NET and Thessaloniki-based ET3). Easily the funniest thing on Greek TV, try and video the news if you can. Absurd, loud and irrelevant music, pompous presenters, outrageous accusations, non-existent stories...you won't be disappointed. As for anonymous witnesses or alleged criminals with their faces digitally covered – nine times out of ten, you can see right through them.

...Here is Alain Delon

TV news is forever giving huge coverage to any film star or super-model in town. No one can justify a *lead* item of 15 minutes on Alain Delon's visit to Greece which is what happened on one station. Watching the telly from his luxury Athens hotel, the French heartthrob must have thought we were taking the Michel.

Note: a) Greece's commercial TV stations, led by Antenna, Mega, Alpha and Star, specialise in acting as the chief negotiator in tense hostage standoffs, the conversations traditionally conducted live on air via mobile phone. 'Do you have any family?' was the not-terribly-bright question put in November 2000 by one news anchorman to Christos Kendiras who had earlier the same day shot his mother-in-law dead, killed his wife's alleged lover – for a jury of male Greeks we're still in the community service ballpark here – and was at that point standing with his shotgun at the front of a busload of 32 hijacked Japanese tourists (it's not known how many photos they took). Another TV journalist then negotiated a peaceful surrender and naturally the man died the next day after reportedly jumping from the seventh floor of Athens police headquarters on Suicide Street, aka Alexandras Avenue. b) Late 2001, at the time of the US strikes, a new TV station, Tempo, broadcast what it billed as 'world exclusive' pictures from Afghanistan, which subsequently turned out to be from the slightly less dangerous Pakistan. Amidst a mighty row, the station said an independent expert had confirmed that the pictures he saw were indeed from Afghanistan. This was 100% true. Unfortunately, the pictures that Tempo showed to the expert were not apparently the pictures that the station had broadcast. Undaunted, the ambitious Tempo, which is based in Athens (or at least it says it is), plans to provide exclusive coverage of the 2002 Winter Olympics in Utah, providing there is sufficient snow on Mount Parnitha. c) Eleni Menengaki married Yiannis Latsios on 23 April 2001 in a ceremony shown live on Antenna news. The bubbly blonde has since dressed more conservatively – in the non-Taliban sense of the word – and her show's ratings have undoubtedly plunged.

Some Day My Bus Will Come

Adam and Eve on tour

Arguments. Romance. Mass asphyxiation. A pensioner chasing his watermelon down the aisle. From the rising of the sun to the closing of the taverna, the best show in town is on a bus near you.

Athens by day and Athens by night. Two totally different cities.

Take the buses. In the morning, the average driver will honk and curse his way across the clogged capital but at night he's one happy man – and I think I know why. Going home at 11pm on the A2 Athens-Voula, it slowly dawned on me that there were in fact *two* people sitting in the driver's seat.

As I looked more closely, my mind told me it simply couldn't be true. Not even Olympic had tried this on their overstaffed planes, where 80% of delays in departing are due to difficulties in fitting the crew on board.

But true it was. Either one very cool passenger was determined to get her money's worth or, more likely, the bus driver had been joined by his girlfriend. If the wife had got on, all hell would have broken loose for there really wasn't room for three.

Watching this couple drive us home, the thought occurred to me that the previous Friday's bus, dangerously packed with what I had automatically assumed to be nightclubbers heading for trendy Voula on the coast, was probably the driver having a birthday party on the cheap. Good for him. These guys don't get paid a fortune yet are incredibly skillful. You try smoking a cigarette, talking on a mobile phone, filling in your betting form, listening to a basketball match on the radio and moving a massive vehicle round a bend, all at the same time. Then do it with one hand. Now try it with one hand while swearing at a motorcyclist.

The biggest problem for drivers is normally right behind them. Their trade union has even distributed leaflets pleading with the public to be nicer to drivers. As soon as Greeks get on a stationary bus at a terminal, they expect it to leave immediately, regardless of the actual timetable. Once moving, they'll start arguing over whether to have the air-conditioning on or keep the windows open. According to the union, more and more drivers have died in recent years 'from strokes and haemorrhage' due to stress and what they term the 'non-understanding of the travelling public'. When Athens had the '99 quake (see Page 36), and a lot of traffic involuntarily swerved, some angry passengers told the driver to stop playing around.

Deep down, the blue bus drivers crave the powers long enjoyed by their rivals in the yellow taxis, war criminals every one. Some will try and charge night-time rates in glorious sunshine. One cheeky cabbie wedged a clever device down his trousers. When tightly squeezed – a mannerism which only taxi drivers can perform in public without attracting undue attention – it rapidly accelerated the meter. Cabbies are still demanding fuel subsidies for their enormous engines, whose distinctive sound is mainly to power the meter.

Bus is better. Fares are not usually distance-related, making this means of transport a real bargain with the added bonus that it doesn't matter what the driver's got underneath his overalls.

Sometimes a bus driver can affect your whole week.

One Monday, a blind driver didn't stop, supposedly because I failed to signal dramatically enough, though you bet I did after he went past. Stupidly, I had thought standing by a bus stop was a sufficient hint.

Same week, on a Wednesday evening, which totally disproves the night-day theory outlined above, a miserable driver told me not to eat an ice cream on the bus. I guess Mr Softy or Mr Whippy ran off with his wife 20 years ago and I secretly agreed with the no-food policy anyway.

Come Friday night, a kind driver pulled to a sharp halt after I signalled in desperation a full 20 metres from the stop. That same bus, later on, couldn't get through two badly parked cars on a main road. A fellow traveller blamed, wait for it, the Albanians. Murderers, burglars and, now, very bad parkers. You heard it here first.

When they're not on strike, bus and coach drivers are the hub of Hellenism, keeping the country moving in its own unique way whatever the circumstances. In December 1998, PAOK supporters blocked a motorway in protest at their soccer club being punished for crowd trouble. Many drivers must be looking forward to a horde of civil engineers invading PAOK's pitch minutes before kick-off in a contractual dispute with a third party over the quality of concrete.

◪ Travelling back from Piraeus one night, and going at tremendous speed around a sharp bend, my articulated bus obviously hit something, to judge by the very loud sound of something obviously being hit.

Without stopping, the driver called out to a group of giggling youngsters at the rear: 'Did we hit anything, kids?' 'Yes,' they replied, and, to give the driver credit, he immediately pulled the bus over, got out and walked back the 80 kilometres (okay, 150 metres) to investigate.

None of us on the bus ever saw him again.

That might be an exaggeration. *Most* of us never saw him again. I waited for 40 minutes, once walking up the road whilst keeping an eye on the stranded bus in case one of the rapidly dwindling group of passengers decided to take his chances at the wheel. Neither then nor the following evening did I see any sign of damage or, for that matter, the driver.

In the end I walked home. To this day I wonder what he hit.

Queen of the Chocolate Drops

Loyalty on legs

Leaving your friends behind for life in a new country is hard. Leaving your family is painful. Leaving your dog is unacceptable. The bad news came in July 1996.

My dog died last week. A vet put her down after diagnosing very severe kidney problems. She was unable to walk and kept falling off her favourite chair. For a dog who had long dominated races up the local field, it must have been very hard.

We got her from a local dog home and immediately my little sister and I argued over the name. I wanted to call her Wesley (after John, the founder of Methodism, my family's religion). Sister Sue, being a few years younger but many decades more sensible, wanted a simple name – and that's what, thankfully, we went for. Scamp. Or Scampi. Or the black-and-white bullet suddenly disappearing after something vastly more interesting than humans. 'S-c-a-m-p-iiiiiiiiii! You come back here right now or I'm going home. Scamp, I'm warning you. Can you hear me Scamp? SCAMP! Where are you? Right, I'm going, I mean it...Please!'

My footballing friends loved her. On first hearing me call out her name, they thought I said 'Scum'. Inevitably, after this, there was always a joyful chorus of cheers whenever 'Scum' appeared on the field.

She lived to be 15, an age which some humans don't make, and scanned an important part of my life. I remember Scamp from school years, going through university (she was a clever dog) and then coming out to Greece in 1992.

In later years, I often spoke pigeon Greek to Scamp and she would woof in appreciation at just how hard this language was. Fluent in chocolate drops, chips and Sunday roast gravy, she could have made a fine career for herself by freelancing as a black-box hunter. Attach a chocolate drop and after any plane crash Scamp would have found it in seconds.

When I heard she was very poorly, it was one of the few times that being far away from England was deeply irritating. Scamp wasn't eating or drinking anything. My mother had to squeeze a sponge around her mouth. The vet wasn't hopeful.

There was a cruel twist the next morning when, just as had happened every day for the past 15 years, my father came downstairs to be greeted by an up-and-walking Scamp, tail wagging, even a woof of welcome. But this was her last goodbye. She quickly got worse that same morning. Off to the vet. And no more S-c-a-m-p-iiiiiiiiii!

She was more my parents' dog than anyone else's – and in particular my Dad's. Both of them took her for thousands of walks but only my father shared major decisions with this faithful mongrel. Dad was distraught at Scamp's death and later wrote very movingly about her. He said he had cried more than when his own father had died. Only readers with a dog currently trying to attract their attention will understand.

Dogs are judged differently to humans but Scamp would do well either way. She never bit anyone, was forever friendly (except to postmen) and made the perfect diplomatic doggie by behaving exactly the same way to all the Basques, Brits and Greeks she came across.

What's more, if truth be told, Scamp always did come back after a few minutes. She just wanted to have a look, that's all.

And there's nothing wrong with that.

ABOUT THE AUTHOR

Brian Church, 36, is a leading commentator on the politics and history of modern Greece, having lived in Athens since last Thursday.

His first book, *Learn Greek in 25 Years - A crash course for the linguistically challenged* (ISBN 960-86395-1-4), also published by the *Athens News*, is still selling atrociously and was accidentally reprinted in July 2000.

Church is currently working on *English for Greeks*, a self-study guide for adults, with his brother Michael, a fully qualified lifeguard.